Unlikely Stories of a Perfect Childhood

A Memoir

Sue Kerr

CLAIRMONT PUBLISHING SERVICES

Unlikely Stories of a Perfect Childhood
A Memoir

Written and illustrated by Sue Kerr.
Cover illustration by Sue Kerr.
Cover design by Jo Constable, Design Space Gallery.

ISBN: 978-1-9991472-0-4

Layout and formatting by:

CLAIRMONT PUBLISHING SERVICES
5720 Prospect Rd New Minas, NS B4N 3K6

First Edition July 2019

For my darling little sisters

Julie, Polly, Maria, and Ange

who all grew up to be warm, kind,

funny, talented women.

PROLOGUE

I had zero intention of writing a book about my childhood and my mother. Zero. The past was over and done with. No point picking at scabs.

But in the end, this is the book that insisted on being written.

After many years of trying and failing to start my bestseller—a novel I believed would be so inspired it would practically write itself—I was sitting, staring at my laptop, paralysed. The voices in my head yammered, as usual. *Loser. You haven't even started. You'll never write a book. You're too old. Nobody cares what you think. Who do you think you are?*

I remember closing my eyes. I remember taking a long deep breath. I remember my throat hot and tight. *Maybe they're right. I'm 54. If I was going to be a writer, I'd be one by now. Maybe it's time to stop pretending...*

And then I heard a new voice. Clear and calm, not to be messed with.

Tell your story.

As if it were the most obvious thing in the world. *My story. I don't think so.*

I resisted. For months. I was not interested in digging up the past. I'd put it behind me. I'd moved on.

But the voice wouldn't stop. It drowned out every other voice in my head.

Tell your story.

As if it were inevitable.

I started. I wrote a story about Mum dying. And one about digging toheroa at Oreti Beach with Dad. About Mum trying to stop me writing a journal when I was sixteen. Mum confiscating my contraceptive pills. So many stories about Mum.

Writing these stories unearthed the resentment, anger, and anxiety I was still carrying around after all these years. Writing brought it all to life again. At first it was painful and emotionally exhausting, but writing helped me make sense of it all. It helped me heal.

I was worried that nobody would believe these stories. They are unlikely, given our family's reputation. By all accounts I'd had a perfect childhood. People who knew us never hesitated to lay it on thick—what a close and happy family; what fun parents; what good times.

What a wonderful life.

I didn't remember it like that. Sure there were plenty of hijinks and antics. And yes we were well-fed and sheltered and educated. We had a stay-at-home Mum. Dad always had a job. We went on picnics and holidays. God knows we were well-dressed.

Those images of a perfect childhood were crystal clear in my mind. And yet my feelings about childhood were an uncomfortable mix of shame, confusion and worry.

Writing these stories has been like shining a light under the bed where the scary monster lurks. Every telling, every edit and rewrite, I realized: There's no monster. There's no shame. There are no villains and no victims. There are just stories. Some sad, some hilarious, some a little bit of both.

I know my memories might not match yours. If there's one thing I've learned about memory—it's utterly subjective. Even if you were in the same room at the same time, you'll have your own version of the story. And your version is as true as mine.

It's OK. We all have our own stories. These unlikely stories are mine.

Chapter 1
TERMINAL

I'm holding her. Her hands and feet are cold. The rest of her body is burning. I'm holding on to my mother so she's not alone when she dies. Earlier today she said she was scared of dying. I think she's unconscious now. But I imagine she's still scared, she'd want company. She always wanted company.

I don't talk to her. I just hold on, feeling her hands and feet get colder, her heart on fire. Part of me is repulsed. But I do it anyway, reminding myself that she held me for nine months inside her own body; she gave birth to me. And I hope that this act, holding her as she dies, will somehow make up for the distance between us.

Her breath gets lighter and lighter. Her whole body cools down. Aunty Angela and Aunty Sally, both nurses, sit next to the bed. They said this will be her last night. It's five in the morning and we've all been awake for what feels like days.

"It's OK, Rosie," one of them whispers. "You can go now. You were always the last one to leave the party."

We laugh, and wait with her. I hold her until she goes.

A month earlier Mum called and told me she had terminal cancer. It was Sunday evening in Vancouver. We had friends over for dinner. It was Monday in New Zealand, and Mum had just come from the hospital. I remember her voice on the phone, strangely small and shaky.

"It's in my lungs. There is nothing they can do. The doctors made me feel I should just lie down and die."

"There must be something they can do. You can't just give up."

"They gave me about a month to live."

"What? They can't just write you off like that. There's got to be something we can do. Let me think about it. I'll call you back tomorrow."

I hung up. I curled up on the couch.

I heard voices from the dinner table, but all I picked up was, "... foetal position."

Bullshit.

I didn't cry. I didn't feel sad. I was appalled. Just lie down and die? Who the hell do these doctors think they are, putting a time limit on someone's life? And why was Mum being so passive, accepting their word for it?

"My mother's dying of her diagnosis," I said to anyone who would listen.

Over the next few days I kept in touch by phone. I couldn't tell for sure what was going on. Mum sounded upbeat and strained at the same time. She'd had her lungs drained at the hospital, and it hurt worse than childbirth. She was drinking wine in bed with Nana and Pat O'Brien. The hospice people were coming for a family meeting. She got a new red satin dressing gown. My sisters and their kids were there for a barbeque. How sick was she? Was death really on her doorstep?

I phoned my youngest sister. "I think you should come," she said. "She's not looking too flash."

I arrived in Invercargill a couple of days later on a windy, hot Tuesday afternoon. Mum wasn't at the airport. That's when it sunk in that she was really sick. She'd never miss an airport pickup if she could help it. I don't remember who picked me up. We went straight to Mum's place.

She was sitting up in bed in her new dressing gown, her blonde bob recently blow-dried, wearing makeup, and looking pretty good, considering. She shot me a coy smile, like a child caught doing something naughty, flashing some charm before facing inevitable trouble. I bent over to kiss her cheek. Her perfume wafted from her hair and shoulders. The perfume maker might claim the scent embodied enchantment, mystery, magic, and exoticism, but to me it just smelled like Mum.

She reached her arms around me. It was a familiar brittle hug. She had never been a soft mother.

"I can't get used to your hair that colour," she laughed, "I could never let my hair go grey. Too aging."

I looked down at her grey roots. She would have been magnificent grey.

"You're looking good, Mum."

"Thanks. I'm not feeling very flash."

A couple of hours later I watched her sleeping. Small grimaces flicking over her face, makeup gone, false teeth loose in her mouth, her leg and knee bones sharp under the dark blue sheets. She was too thin, and she looked older than I'd ever seen her, but still younger than her 59 years. Mum had always looked younger than she was. In three weeks the cancer would grip her so harshly she'd look older than her own mother.

She stirred, opened her eyes, looked around, cautious, suspicious.

"What are you doing here?"

"I arrived today, Mum. I flew in from Vancouver."

"Am I going to die?" Eyes darting around the room now.

"That's what the doctors said, Mum. That's what you've been saying."

She stares at me, eyes huge. "Will I see Peter?"

Peter's my father. He died in this same room, maybe even the same bed, almost ten years ago. He was only 54.

"Maybe you'll see Dad. You're older than him now."

"So I am… Am I going to die?"

"I don't know, Mum."

"Who's going to look after Michael?"

Michael and Mum married a couple of years after Dad died. He'd been a bachelor for 56 years. He'd brag that he'd got a wife, five step-daughters, five grandchildren and a mother-in-law all in one shot. He never dreamed he'd lose his wife of only eight years to lung cancer. She'd been healthy as a horse, never smoked. He expected her to outlive him by a mile. We all did.

"We'll all look after Michael."

"Am I dying, Susan? Am I really?"

I did the only thing I felt I was good at. I took over the household—herding visitors and helpers, arranging flowers, changing bedsheets, answering the phone and the door. I talked to doctors, lawyers and accountants, made tea for crying relatives, met with the hospice workers, coordinated offers of help so we had enough casseroles and cakes to feed us every day, but not too many. I heard someone say I was running the place like I ran my business. I took it as a compliment. *Just like Dad would have done it.*

In spite of my domestic take-over, anyone could see that command central was still up in Mum's room. She dictated who could visit her and when. She approved or rejected the flower arrangements for her room. She would eat only canned peaches. She made us return a yellow box of tissues to the supermarket and get pink or blue. "You know I hate yellow."

And then the morphine arrived.

Morphine gave Mum more physical vigour—she was no longer racked with pain—but it slushed her mind. Every time I went into her room now, she'd get upset, "I have to go home, Susan. I can't die in Canada. You've got to take me home!"

I'd pull back the curtains. "You're home, Mum, in your house in Invercargill. Look how lovely your roses are this year."

"Don't trick me!"

"I'm not tricking you, Mum. Look at your garden. Your roses. They're beautiful."

"Oh…"

She'd fall asleep. If I was in the room when she woke up, she'd rail again.

"I have to go home to die. I don't want to die in Canada."

"You're not in Canada, Mum, you're at home."

"What are you doing here?"

"I'm visiting you, Mum, in Invercargill. Look out the window."

"Let me go home."

For a couple of days she hallucinated about sewing. She sat up in bed pulling an invisible needle back and forth, back and forth, through invisible

cloth. Then she'd drop the needle in the bed and insist on finding it.

Getting her in and out of bed was an ordeal. But she would not be talked out of it. She was going to find that damned needle if it killed her.

I thought it might help to play along, so I searched the bed with her.

"Here it is, Mum, here's your needle." I held out my hand, expecting her to take the invisible needle and get back to her sewing.

"You little bitch," she snarled, grabbing my wrist, "Get me out of Canada. Let me go home!"

All I could do was cry. It was the first time she'd seen me cry since I got home.

"Come here," she said, "I'll comfort you."

But I didn't want to go to her. I felt an old, familiar dread. I was a confused child, in awe of my mother and terrified of her. I didn't know if she'd hug me or shove me away.

I sat in Old Grannie's rocking chair in the bay window, out of reach, but in full view of my mother. I watched and waited. She got thinner, older, smaller every day.

Out the patio door, all you could see were roses. Big, buxom, almost rude the way they flowered so relentlessly that year. Giant pink and white and mauve roses, crawling all over the fences, flopping into the neighbours' yards, lavish and unashamed. Saying goodbye, maybe, to Mum, to Rosemary, who loved her roses big and blousy.

The January sunshine was harsh by mid-morning. Mum would ask us to close the curtains. So we'd sit with her in the cool half dark, spears of white gold sunlight slashing through the gloom from under the drawn curtains.

There's a picture of that room, with its carefully matching colours and patterns, burned into my brain. Blues, pinks and greys, the blue satin bedspread an exact match for the tiny diamond shapes dotting the silver-grey carpet. Navy blue sheets, white cotton pillow cases with ruffled edges. Full-length heavy curtains, swirling with flowers in the same blues and a splash of pink, draped over the white lace sheers.

The furniture is dark wood, antique. There's the dresser with three oval mirrors and tiny drawers with brass keyholes but no keys. The dresser is covered with Mum's antique auction finds, a rough carved wooden jewellery box, a dainty cut-crystal bowl, a pair of brass candle sticks with no candles, an ornate oval silver picture frame with Dad smiling out of it, his blue and white striped shirt another perfect match for the decor.

There were cushions to match the curtains, antique bedside lamps on brass stands, silk flowers in crystal vases, faded prints of cute old-fashioned girls, their hair in ringlets. And Old Grannie's rocking chair. Dad rescued it one Saturday morning from the back of a truck headed to the dump. That went down in family history as one of our luckiest saves. An ancient wooden rocking chair tossed out with the rubbish after Old Grannie died. Mum upholstered it in soft blue velvet, and set it, just so, in the bay window.

I sat in that rocking chair, drowning in blue, pink and grey, longing to go home to my simple airy apartment with its books and plants, where nothing much matched at all.

If you'd walked into that bedroom, you'd notice Mum propped up on a pile of pillows, looking much thinner, much more gaunt than the last time you'd seen her, even though it had only been a couple of days. You'd notice I was pale and quiet in the rocking chair. You'd assume I was suffering a huge grief, overwhelming distress. You might have said, "It's so sad for you girls, losing your mother so young. You'll miss her so much."

And I would have sighed, said nothing, and you would never have known the truth.

I didn't know the truth. I didn't even know what I was feeling. Except numb. Numb was nothing new. I'd always been numb. Numb-ish. Especially around Mum. *Mum rhymes with numb.*

I must have been feeling something. Nobody sits beside their dying mother and feels nothing, do they? I didn't feel any grief. When Dad died I got to know the black sucking suffocating undertow of grief.

No, I didn't feel grief. Something was wrong. I was watching my mother die and I had no tenderness for her. No soft feelings. Nothing that felt like love.

I was certainly making a good impression, sitting at her bedside for hours on end. I did practical things, the kind of things I'd do for anyone who was dying. I helped wash and feed her. I tended to her needs. *Tended sounds like tender.*

But it wasn't. I did things that looked a lot like tenderness and love. But I felt nothing. Most of the time I just sat and waited. Wondering when I'd start feeling sad.

Chapter 2
PARTIES, PICNICS, & PRANKS

Perhaps I'm giving the impression I was alone with Mum. I wasn't. My dear uncle Jim, Dad's brother, came up to Vancouver from California as soon as he heard I was going to see Mum, and came to New Zealand with me. Two of my father's sisters, both nurses, came and stayed with us so we could keep Mum at home while she died. David came down from Vancouver as soon as he could.

Three, sometimes four or five of us looked after Mum around the clock. Every day the house filled with friends and family—my four younger sisters and their children; Mum's seven siblings and her mother; nieces, nephews, cousins, aunts and uncles from both sides of the family; Mum's many friends—they came in waves, all day every day. People from the church brought her Communion. Apologetic business people came on last-minute errands, to tidy up the will, rearrange bank accounts. The priest heard her Confession and gave her the Last Rites so she was all set to go to heaven. But mostly we were surrounded by friends and relatives.

Mum was the most popular person I've ever known. She charmed people, gave them a good time. Bubbly, so much fun, such a good sort. That's what people said about her. They say it even now, all these years later. "Rosie was always such good fun. Such a good sort. So bubbly."

Hundreds of people came to visit. It seemed as if everyone our family had ever known dropped what they were doing and came to see Mum before she died. When I first arrived, her room was often full of people; she seemed like her old self, holding court, joking and laughing. But as the days passed, she had less and less energy. One or two visitors could sit for a few minutes on the side of her bed, hold her hands, talk quietly, or pray—that was all the socializing she could cope with.

The visitors kept coming. We'd greet them at the front door, ask them to wait in the kitchen—or the lounge if the kitchen was full. We'd tell whoever was sitting with Mum their time was up, and ask Mum if she would see the friend or aunt, next on the list, first come first served. She'd nod, and we'd usher one set of guests away, and escort the next batch up to her room.

Sometimes she'd refuse to see a visitor—if she considered them "too morbid and depressing". This presented a diplomatic problem, but we managed it. Mum would eventually go to sleep, and then we could sneak in the morbid and depressing, whispering, "Just for a couple of minutes. We can't wake her.

If you want to leave a message or a note, we'll make sure she gets it."

Those of us staying at the house had an informal roster: sit with Mum, look after the waiting visitors, or sleep. We shared the only spare bed in the house, one getting in as the other got out. The sheets were always warm.

We decided we needed a daily meeting, to make sure everyone was doing OK, to pass on instructions from the hospice people. Mostly we needed to relax, let off steam.

We asked close friends to sit with Mum for an hour at 6pm each day while we had a family get-together.

It was the second day. We were on our second round of drinks, having a good laugh, when the kitchen door swung open and in strode Mum in her red dressing gown, bare feet, her head held high. She slowed just long enough to shoot us a coy but knowing look, before striding through the kitchen, out the back door, and into the garden.

We all jumped up, tripping over each other as we tried to stop her. She hadn't stood up on her own for days. Nobody knew she could still walk. She was a vital ghost—not there, but very much there—letting us know that she may be dying, but she wasn't dead yet. This was still her house, and don't forget it.

I realize now how much she would have hated being stuck in bed when there were people down the other end of the house, in *her* kitchen, having a drink and a laugh without her. Mum came alive, sparkled, when she entertained—that was the Rosie everyone knew and loved.

But she didn't join us that day. She couldn't. She had just enough life left in her to walk out into her garden, get her bare feet into the cool grass, take one last look at her roses. Someone caught up with her and helped her back to bed. I think that was the last time she got up.

When we were growing up there were always parties. I can still hear the muffled rumble from the other end of the house, a soundtrack to our childhood: jumbled talking and laughing, a shout, a car pulling up the driveway, a car door slamming, the doorbell ding-dong, all muted by our closed bedroom door, the long hallway, the closed kitchen door. And the dark. Julie, Polly and me—tucked up in our cosy beds with matching flannelette sheets, in our matching pyjamas with our hot water bottles—in the big bedroom at the far end of the house. Who was at the party? What were they laughing at? What were they doing? We didn't know. We didn't dare get up.

Sounds escape from the kitchen when the door opens—a favourite uncle's voice, a name we recognise, a familiar laugh. Who's coming up the hall? We hear a stumble and laugh, or a swear. We never see them, never know who it is. We're supposed to be asleep. And we do sleep, eventually, exhausted from trying to stay awake.

When we get up in the morning, the visitors are gone, the house is clean and quiet. Like nothing happened at all.

On weekends our house was overrun with visitors. It seemed like that, but it can't be true. We spent a lot of the weekend out visiting. It was normal for families to drive around and drop in to visit relatives and friends. Nothing was planned. You'd hear the crunch of car tires on the gravel drive, the bang of car doors, the ring of the doorbell and a voice calling, "Oooo Hooo". And no matter what had been happening in the house, we'd swing into hospitality mode. Everyone was welcomed. We kids were expected to entertain the visiting children—whether we liked them or not—by including them in our games and activities. Dad would pour drinks for the adults. And we're on track for a party.

I was older than most of my cousins and the family friends' children, so I was mostly spared the agony of forced socializing. I was quite happy to slip into my room and read or write. When we had visitors, nobody bothered me to "stop being anti-social and come downstairs," so I never thought of these visits as an invasion, but that's what they looked like.

These visits could evolve into hours-long events. Afternoon drinks would drag into dinner time. The dads would all put in money and someone would phone in a huge order to the local fish and chip shop. Kids would bike down to pick up the order. We'd open the steaming newspaper packages on the living room floor and eat as much as we liked—there always seemed to be enough. When the last chip was gone, the last drop of tomato sauce licked up, there would be rowdy games of hide and seek. Twister. Challenges and jokes. Noise and laughter.

As the night drew on, the boy cousins would agitate for Dad to "flush them down the toilet". They'd poke him and annoy him, till he grabbed them, carried them by the ankles into the bathroom, dangled their heads over the toilet and pulled the chain. They'd scream with delight. He never did that to the girls. This was the Uncle Peter special, just for boys.

In the house on Patterson Street, we didn't have a flush toilet until I was nine. We had an outhouse—a shed made of corrugated iron with a bucket toilet inside—called the dunny. Dad would wait till one of the visitors went out to relieve themselves, then he'd sneak out the back door and throw stones or rocks, scaring the poor person inside half to death with the deafening clang of rock on metal. He'd throw fire crackers at the dunny if the party was going particularly well.

On Sundays after Mass there'd often be a picnic. Carloads of families, friends and relatives, at the beach, at a river or a lake. The dads unbolted the seats from the car floors and set them up on the ground like an outdoor living room. The mothers spread out tartan

blankets, boxes filled with cold meat, tomatoes, buttered white bread, apples, cake, a thermos of tea. Dad would sink his flagon of beer into the river or a rock pool to keep it cold.

Always the same. Kids running wild, flying. Adults sitting by the cars, talking, laughing, drinking. We'd drift back, they'd give us a sandwich or a drink, and shoo us away. "Go away and play, you kids." We'd drift off, drift back. Each time we returned, their conversation was louder, more hilarious. They'd let us get our own food; they'd stop caring if we hung around.

They'd start playing games, competitions, limbo and three-legged races. There would be dares. Bets. Wrestling. More and more laughing. Someone would be tossed into the water, fully dressed. Instamatic cameras would flash. We would stop our roaming, and watch. Thrilled, worried. One or the other.

When the food ran out, when it started to get dark, we'd all pack into the cars for home. We'd have a bath to wash off the sand and mud. Calamine lotion on the sunburn. Matching pyjamas. Eggs and toast for dinner. Off to our cosy beds, worn out.

Our childhood. A long-running production of picnics, visits, and parties. We kids bobbed along in the current.

The evening of Mum and Dad's 13th wedding anniversary got off to a bad start when Dad disappeared and we thought he'd died, perhaps even killed himself.

He went upstairs after dinner to take a shower. Nothing unusual about that. When he didn't come back downstairs, Mum sent one of us up to check that he was OK. But he wasn't there. The bathroom window was wide open, and there was no Dad. He must have fallen out. Or jumped. We were too afraid to go outside with a torch to look.

Mum sent me across the street to get our neighbour, Ambrose. Ambrose was good in a crisis. He checked the back yard. He didn't find the body. We all looked at him. What to do next? Call the police? Call the priest? Mum started crying. Or was it one of the little kids? Probably both.

We all jumped at the loud knock at the back door, the urgent ringing of the doorbell. We rushed to open it. A familiar-looking priest stood there, grinning. A huge banging of pots and pans, and a hoard of people dressed in costumes rushed towards us into the house.

"Peter, you stupid bastard," Mum yelled at the priest, "we thought you'd jumped out the bathroom window."

Why was the priest our father? Why was he laughing when we thought he was dead?

"You kids, go on upstairs. Dad's OK. It's just a joke. It's a surprise party," Mum beamed. Surprise parties were her favourite. We went to sleep to the muffled thud of partying in the rooms downstairs, underneath our bedrooms.

I remember a few years later waking up in the middle of the night, startled by a herd of people thundering up the stairs yelling at the tops of their voices. I heard Mum scream and Dad swear. I heard water gushing into the bathtub, more screams from Mum and Dad's bedroom. I crept out onto the landing. My sisters peeked from behind their bedroom doors. We saw Father McLean and a bunch of strangers drag Mum into the bathroom in her nightie. We heard her scream again when they dumped her into the cold water. Dad was leaning on their bedroom door frame howling with laughter. Then Father McLean and the other people charged out of the bathroom, back down the stairs, slamming the front door behind them. Gone as fast as they'd arrived.

"Get back into bed you kids! It's just a joke." Mum dripped across the landing, glaring at Dad still laughing.

What happened? Why was Father McLean here in the middle of the night throwing Mum in the bath? Snuggling into my still-warm sheets, I realized we'd brought this on ourselves. We'd asked for it.

That afternoon, Father McLean had been visiting. We had other visitors too, family friends with lots of kids.

"Will you stay for a meal tonight, Father?"

"Sorry Rosie, I've got a better offer—dinner out and then cards at the presbytery with the A-team."

Some of the priests socialized with parishioners—drinking, playing cards, small-stakes gambling—and there was plenty of rivalry going on. Father McLean played cards with two groups, the A-team and the B-team. My parents and their friends were the B-team.

"That's too bad Father. I was going to cook something special for you. I'm a much better cook than anyone on the A-team!"

"Well why don't you make us a nice supper for after cards?"

"The cheek of you!" Mum snorted. "If we're not good enough to play cards with you tonight, we're not going to feed you!"

They bantered on. After Father left, Mum and her friend Mary laughed about how cheeky he'd been. They really should get him back.

"You kids go and get a big bowl of grass and weeds, and find as many worms and slugs as you can in the compost. Someone, go to Dad's shed and find a piece of wood about the size of a banana loaf."

The younger kids ran out, delighted. I wasn't sure this was a great idea, so I stayed put.

"Susan, you ring the presbytery and tell Father McLean the B-team will supply supper after all. If he's not home, leave a message with the housekeeper. Tell them we'll bring it around and leave it in his kitchen."

I left the message with the housekeeper. Mum, Mary and the other kids made a big tray of grass, weed, slug and worm sandwiches, on thin white buttered bread. Mum used her electric knife to trim off the crusts and cut the sandwiches into perfect triangles. She arranged them neatly on a plate and covered them with plastic wrap. Just like the real thing. We gave the block of wood a lavish coat of chocolate icing, and decorated it with frills and rosettes using Mum's cake decorating kit, usually reserved for icing birthday cakes. Then Mum and Mary delivered supper to the presbytery.

"God bless the B-team for making us a great supper," Father declared when he saw the goodies. We heard this later, from an A-team eyewitness.

Father ate a sandwich or two every time he went into the kitchen to fill up the drinks. It wasn't until one of the A-team ladies tried to cut the cake that they realized they'd been tricked. There weren't many sandwiches left by then. It was only fair for them to come over to our place and get Mum back.

This was the way of things. Mum and Dad were popular, sociable and hospitable. They had a knack for fun and games. Our house was a magnet for visitors. It was noisy and chaotic with practical jokes, pantomimes, competitions.

Mum particularly excelled at the hilarity. I can still see her sitting at the piano playing Moonlight Sonata in the wrong key at double speed. Moonlight Sonata and Norwegian Lullaby. They were her only two tunes. Double speed, off key. She'd beam, looking over her shoulder like Liberace. If there was a decent lampshade around, she'd be wearing it on her head.

There was never a social occasion without drinking. Alcohol was a permanent feature in our lives.

You know how some people obsess about having a spare tire and an emergency beacon in the boot of the car at all times? We had to have a crate of beer in our car boot. At all times. Most people who shop at the liquor store come home with a bag or a box of bottles. We took a trailer to Wilson Neill to buy our booze. My sister Maria remembers thinking we were very special Wilson Neill customers because they sent us a huge box of El Dorado chocolates every Christmas. Most families have a bottle recycling bin. We had a bottle recycling shed. This was our normal.

The week before Dad died he was in hospital, recovering from the operation that confirmed he had advanced cancer in many of his internal organs. There was nothing for the doctors to do but close up the incision and tell Dad he didn't have long to live—a month or two at the outside. He only lasted three weeks.

I was sitting alone with him about 6pm when the duty nurse popped into the cubicle to pick up his empty dinner tray.

"Would you two like a beer? We've got Steinlager in the fridge."

"Don't you know I'm dying of liver cancer?" Dad laughed.

"Yes, of course I do! A beer's not going to do any more harm now."

And then Dad said, rather sadly, "You know, this is the first time in my life I really don't feel like drinking beer."

Only two days before he died—he was back home by then—he said, "Susie, have a look in the bottom drawer of the bedside cabinet. There's an envelope there."

It was full of cash. A few hundred dollars.

"Go down to Wilson Neill and buy plenty of booze for my funeral. I don't want it to run out. And get plenty of sparkling wine for Mum."

I sat in the rocking chair, gripping a coffee mug full of Merlot. I felt the wine flooding a welcome slack down my neck and into my shoulders, down my arms and legs, into my fingers and toes, carrying off, magically, the weight of what was happening, the pain, the confusion. I drank from a mug so Mum wouldn't know it was wine. She loved wine. Not red. Sparkling white wine was her drink. It must have bubbles. Once she exploded a SodaStream bottle trying to "fizz up" some chardonnay to make it bubbly.

When she first started to get sick, to notice something odd going on in her back and chest she told us she felt like there was a fizzing inside her lungs, like she was breathing out bubbles.

"It's all that San Bernadino you've been drinking, Mum!" That sounds cruel as I write it. I wish I'd said *don't be sick, Mum. Don't die.*

The morphine pump purred. I read somewhere it was easy to adjust the dose on those pumps, make it an overdose, for a quick and painless death. I thought about it, for just a few seconds. Then I remembered Mum striding through the kitchen, so tall, strong, muscular, powerful. She wasn't, of course. She was thin and wasted. But in that moment, all her life force had surged back into her body, and it was frightening. She was frightening. Still.

Chapter 3
DUM AND MAD

There is so much help, so much kindness around us.

Hospice nurses come every morning to check Mum, bathe her, top up the morphine pump. Two of Dad's sisters, both nurses, are staying with us. They know terminal cancer; they tell us what we're seeing, the signs, the way death steps closer each day. My sisters come every day. Our aunts and Mum's friends bring us the food we love, beautiful flowers from their gardens. An uncle brings a lawn mower and mows the lawns. We want for nothing, except normality.

When I need a break, I borrow a car and drive to Oreti Beach. The sand is packed so flat, so hard, you can drive on the beach for miles. Even in midsummer you take a coat to Oreti Beach. A hat and scarf too. I pull a wad of tissues from the box on the passenger seat, and stuff it up my sleeve. I need to cry. I should cry. But I can't. Maybe here.

Oreti Beach. Huge wild grey-blue sky, churning grey-green surf, hard grey-black sand. White streaks fizz along the top of the breakers. Gulls, white smears in the sky, white dots on the sand.

I walk into the endless Southerly wind, fists punched deep into my coat pockets, shoulders hiked up around my ears. This is how we walk in Southland. *Home. Where I come from.*

I am the only one here today, but I see generations on this beach. Rows of grinning children in puffy rompers and frilly bonnets. Mothers and grandmothers sitting on the sand, their dresses stretched across their modest folded knees, their bloomers showing anyway. A grandfather, impossibly formal in a suit, tie and hat. At Oreti Beach for a day out.

I can see Mum and Dad, not married, not even dating yet, with a group of friends swimming out past the breakers. They all see the black fins charging towards them through the heaving green swell. They all thrash back to the safety of the sand. Mum's terrified. Dad comforts her. That's when their friends know there will be something between them. Porpoises, not sharks. They swim back out.

Look over there. Dad and his friends drag a flounder net through the low-tide shallows. Mum paces the wet sand, wrapped up against the wind in a man's overcoat. A friend asks Dad, "When did Rosie have the baby?" I wouldn't be born for three more weeks. I didn't show. A deep disappointment to Mum, who more than anything wanted to look pregnant with her first baby. The day after the positive pregnancy test she bought yards of fabric to make the voluminous maternity smocks I failed to fill out.

And see, back there, in the shelter of the sand hills, a clump of cars, parked around a picnic site. Adults nursing their drinks, endless talking and laughing. Kids running wild back and forth between the water and the sand hills and home base. A cousin drops their sandwich, and we feed it, limp and gritty, to the circling screaming gulls. Someone knocks over a bottle of beer, a father curses, and we all stop to watch the sand suck it up, leaving only the foam behind.

Look, there's Dad again, walking slowly backwards in the wet sand, head down, scanning left right, left right. Every few steps he stops, bends down, draws a circle in the sand with the red pencil he keeps tucked behind his ear. A gaggle of kids follow along, to find the pencil marks, each ringing a pea-sized black hole in the sand.

We dig quietly. He has taught us how to sneak up on the toheroa, the elusive shellfish that lives deep in the wet sand at Oreti Beach. Our tiny hands shovel sand gently; a cold silty pool forms around our arms as we dig. When we finally touch the sharp edge of the blueish shell, up to our elbows by now in freezing water, we stop and yell, "Dad!" He comes running, get out of his way, plunges his big man hands down the hole and grabs the sucking

toheroa before it gets away, plops it into the black plastic bucket.

We want to catch the toheroa ourselves of course, and sometimes he lets us try. But our small girl hands are no match for those slick sucking shellfish—they're far too fast and strong. Dad's system is best. He's thought it through.

On these trips to the beach there are not just the five of us girls in the car. We're allowed to bring as many friends as we can cram in. Mum can't come because she takes up too much room. Dad wants numbers.

I might be exaggerating, but it seems like he piles us into the back seat, biggest kids first, with a layer of smaller kids on top. At least three in the front passenger seat. Some even crouch on the floor under the dashboard. He drives us slowly, his wiggling giggling cargo, to the beach. The quota is ten toheroa per person. Dad finds, circles and pulls them all. I didn't know until much later, when the toheroa population was almost gone, we kids were only there to boost the quota.

We came out here to Oreti Beach the day Dad died. Almost ten years ago. He stopped breathing about five in the morning. The doctor came at seven. The undertaker collected his body at eight. "We'll bring him back in the coffin this afternoon." There would be a wake at the house. But before the wake, right that minute, there was a colossal emptiness in the house. Dad was gone.

"Let's go to the beach." As if that's where he'd be. As if that's where we'd find him. But no. He wasn't there. The wind shoved us around that day. The rain spat in our faces.

Today he's here. Not in any physical way. He's here in the memories, painted all over the sand, the sky, the water. Some are clear as the day they happened. Some happened long before I was born; technically I can't remember them. But I do remember. From the stories told over and over, from the old black and white photos. Those are my memories too. Passed down, second hand maybe, but good memories.

I turn around and let the wind steer me back to the car. Dad would have loved it here today. The empty beach is a rash of fat black toheroa holes.

It's eerie quiet back at the house. No visitors. Mum's eyes are closed.

"I went out to the beach, Mum. For a walk. I was the only one there."

She says nothing. But maybe she can hear.

Dad looked over from his silver frame on the dresser. He seemed to smile at me, kindly, the way he used to smile at me when he was alive, a shy smile; nobody else would see it. A recognition. That smile said, "How did two sensible people like us end up in a crazy family like this?"

I sit in the rocking chair, with Mum to my right on the bed, and Dad to my left in the picture frame. Mum and Dad. Dum and Mad I can't help thinking. Julie once recited her brilliant spontaneous verse at the dinner table, "Mum is dum and Dad is mad." She got in trouble—with Mum. Dad thought it was funny. Dad used to say, "Rosie, it's a good thing the girls got your looks and my brains. Other way round would have been a Total Disaster."

Mum and Dad. Dum and Mad. *Where we came from.*

When we were little Mum would send Julie, Polly and me to the corner to meet Dad's bus after work and walk him home. We were to wait at the bus stop, and stand well back from the curb, so we didn't get run over. When Dad got off the bus, I would take his briefcase. Julie would hold one hand, Polly the other, and we'd walk him the half block home. No other kids met their fathers at the bus like this; I assumed that meant that we loved our father more.

When we got home, Mum would take his coat, Julie would bring his slippers, Polly would escort him to his armchair, and I would bring him his beer. I knew how to pour a perfect beer by the time I was six. Dad taught me to hold the glass on an angle, and let the beer run from the bottle down the side of the glass. No glugging. Go slow, and straighten the glass up as you pour. You want a nice clear amber for most of the glass, less than a half-inch of foam on top. I took my beer pouring very seriously.

We would all sit on or around Dad while he relaxed with a beer after work. It was important to look after Dad, Mum said, because he has to work so hard for everything for us girls—our house, our clothes, our food, holidays, school uniforms, music lessons.

Sometimes in this memory we sit by the roaring fire. Other times we're in shorts and t-shirts, sitting outside. There are no slippers in summer. But there's always beer. Same routine. Mum announces Dad will be home soon. We put away our toys, our homework. We wash our hands and faces, straighten our hair and clothes. Then we go to the corner to meet the bus.

Eventually Dad became the office manager, drove a car to work, and we stopped meeting the bus. We stopped delivering the slippers and the beer. A new routine evolved. Dad would come home from work, change out of his suit and tie into soft corduroy pants and a plaid shirt, then he'd come downstairs and pour drinks for himself and Mum. Dad sat on one of the bar stools just inside the kitchen door with his beer—a large bottle and a real beer glass. Mum was on the other side of the counter with a sherry or a wine. Dinner was almost ready. She'd have tidied herself up before Dad got home, put on some lipstick maybe, brushed her hair.

I can see Mum and Dad as if they were still there, drinking in that kitchen. They weren't drunks, my parents. But they were devoted to the ritual of pouring drinks, raising glasses. We saw this every day growing up. We looked up to it. We thought it was glamourous. Our parents actually did something vaguely romantic, almost like going on a date together every day, right in front of our eyes.

My friends' parents didn't do this, and I thought my parents were somehow superior for it. Some fathers went to the pub right after work, rolled home for dinner, and fell asleep snoring in their armchairs. Some parents didn't drink at all. The father just read the newspaper. The mother just cooked. The family just ate dinner.

My parents had their drinks date, brought their glasses to the dinner table, poured another round. We'd all sit around after dinner, talking and debating. Or bating each other. It was a mini-party every day of the week at our place.

On my 18th birthday, Dad walked in the back door after work, with a brown paper bag in his hand. "Susie, I've bought some wine for your birthday. You're old enough to have a drink with us now." And so I was admitted to the glamourous routine of drinks before dinner. This was my pass to adulthood—a glass with a stem, filled with cheap sweet white wine. Nothing else changed in my relationship with Mum and Dad. But I was allowed to drink with them.

One of my earliest memories is sitting on Dad's knee. I'm on his left knee, facing my little sister Julie perched on his right knee. His shirt is white. No tie. Mahogany brown corduroy pants. His left arm strong around my tiny frame, his right arm around Julie. Julie and I pass his beer back and forth, dipping our top lip into the glass, making white foam moustaches, laughing, licking the bitter drips, quick, catch them before they run down our chins and stain our dresses. We're all laughing.

Dad is small, solid, hard when you hug him. There's no give in him. Nothing soft. Except his hair, dark and curly. He lets us sit on him while we search his head for grey hairs. He pays us a cent for every ten grey hairs we hunt down. But if we pull out a black one, we get no money at all. Just the grey ones. He says it doesn't hurt. But I think it must hurt. We pull hard, we feel the ping as the hairs pop out of his scalp before we drop them onto the pile in his open hand, and he keeps count.

Dad stands us on his knees, holds our hands while he taps his feet, first gently so we balance and giggle, then wilder, we bounce until we shoot up and off into outer-space and he catches us, wheeeee, and we land like graceful gulls at his feet.

And now I remember Julie and me, fresh out of the bathtub in our clean matching pyjamas, toes warming in front of the brick fireplace pulsing orange and yellow embers. Mum is making us toasty pies in the fire—thin white buttered toast filled with hot strings of melted cheese and vegemite or canned spaghetti. Whatever flavour we want. We'll eat them watching a Disney show on TV.

"Susie's only three, but she can read."

Yes, I can read. I'm delighted, dancing and clapping.

Dad is delighted too. "Hold up a record, and she'll read you the title."

Someone holds up the record with the red label. I point. "Little… Red… Hen?"

YES!

The yellow label. "Little. Black. Sambo?"

YES!

Green. "Henny Penny!"

Blue. "Peter and the WOLF!"

Everyone is amazed and clapping, and I am dancing and happy.

How long did Dad and I get away with this party trick? I'm not sure, but ever since I was three, I thought I could read, and I never thought otherwise. As I write this memory I realise too that I knew Dad was on my side. We were a team, even back then.

"I need to see Father McLean. And Nana. I need to talk to her." Mum thrashed in her sheets, trying to sit up. I jumped up to help her.

"OK. I'll ring them. When do you want them to come?"

"Now."

I phoned the priest first, and then Nana, Mum's mother.

Father McLean asked us to leave the room. They do that for a final Confession.

"Are you going to forgive her for the slug and worm sandwiches, Father?"

He chuckled. "I forgave her for that years ago."

I went out into the garage where it was cool. Where I could be alone. The grey filing cabinet door hung open. A humble home for the good wine. I'd kill for a wine. But it's only two o'clock.

It still felt like Dad's garage. His tools and building equipment still hanging where he left them.

The day before he died, I was sitting on the bed with him, propped up against the headboard in a big pile of pillows. He was stretched out flat on his back under the sheets. He looked awful. His skin was yellow. Bright yellow from the liver cancer. He was drawn and thin. He looked like he was made out of plastic. He'd been sleeping, then his eyes opened and he smiled at me.

"You know Susie, there's only one thing I regret in my life."

I perked up. Hoping for something deep and meaningful.

"I haven't dry-walled the garage. I should have done that months ago."

Nobody bothered to do it after he died. What was the point? I stood with my arms wide and spun around, the whole room blurring. A glint up by the ceiling stopped me. Dad's attic ladder. I'd forgotten about the attic.

I pulled the rope attached to the bottom rung, and the aluminium ladder unfolded down to my feet. I climbed up, heaved the wooden trap-door open, and pulled myself up into the gloom. I could hear Father mumbling under my feet. Maybe saying the Last Rites. If I press my ear to the floor, will I hear her last Confession? *Stop it. Leave her alone.*

Every house Dad built had a small hideaway, his space, where he worked on his building plans, listened to the horse racing on his transistor radio, marking the results in the Turf Digest with that red pencil from behind his ear. I wonder what happened to his transistor. I'd like to have it.

Dad built this house; his plans and sketches were still on the floor beside the old unpainted wooden desk, along with a roll of old graph paper, grubby under ten years of dust. His pencils and rulers were still on the desk. It was like he'd climbed down the ladder to get a cup of coffee, and forgot to come back.

The attic was gloomy, primitive. Plywood floor, Pink Batts insulation in the roof. The only curtain on the window beside the desk was a tangle of dusty spider webs. A bare lightbulb hung from a white extension cord. I switched it on.

I had a sudden memory of being up here after Dad's funeral. Looking through boxes. Mum came up the ladder. She'd been crying for days. She was shocked, broken. "I don't know what do to," she bawled. "I don't know how to do anything. Peter did everything." I couldn't bear this. I suppose all she needed was someone to hug her. But I couldn't. All I could do was vow to myself, "I'll never be that dependent on a man." I'm not proud of that moment. *So harsh.*

Ten years later, Mum was dying, and I was back up in the attic. Still feeling harsh.

The attic was strewn with boxes and bags stuffed with Christmas decorations, old books and blankets, clothes and camping gear. Some of my things were up here, in boxes pushed back into the eaves, right on top of Mum's room. I inched them out, as quietly as I could, not wanting to disturb her or alarm Father McLean.

My boxes were full of books, letters, birthday cards, rolled up posters, school report cards and year books. I found my first journal, a hardbound notebook I bought with my pocket money when I was 15.

I took it over to Dad's desk and sat down. The spine was broken. Faded biro drawings gouged the dirty blue cover. The handwriting on the first page was neat, tight. Small.

"I bought this book tonight because I'm sick of keeping some things bottled up in me, things I don't want to tell people, and what better person to tell than myself. At least I understand the situation properly… I don't want this to be a record of the day's events, but a record of my thoughts as well, of things that it's easier to write down than to say to someone… If someone has the mind to read this, I guess it is up to them, but people are entitled to their own private thoughts and secrets and I feel that right should be respected… I would be disappointed in the character of the person who would read further than this…"

That made me smile—even then I knew privacy was a problem; I expected Mum to find and read that journal.

The pages fill up. The handwriting gets loose, flows for a week or two. Tightens up. The journal gets cryptic. Reverts to code. Stops. All in the space of six months in 1976.

We lived in the big old house on Princes Street then. It was so big I got to have my own bedroom. I remember sitting at the desk Mum painted orange to match the yellow and orange daisy-chain wallpaper and the orange and white striped curtains. Mum and Dad decorated all our rooms in that house before we moved in—they wallpapered, painted, made curtains. Everything matched. I loved my room, orange and yellow.

I've finished my homework, and I'm writing in my journal, tending wounds, unpicking conversations, wondering, dreaming. Writing is how I make sense of everything, how I understand my life.

I hear the living room door bang shut. A little sister bunny hops up the stairs and across the landing, stops outside my door.

"Hey Susie!"

"What?"

"Mum says you have to come downstairs and be part of the family."

"No, I can't. I'm busy writing."

"OK." She jumps across the landing, hops down the stairs, two at a time, back into the living room.

The living room door opens again. Closes a bit too quickly. Adult footsteps, one on each stair, a squeak on the third step from the top. Five paces across the landing, and Mum throws open my bedroom door.

"What are you doing up here? Come downstairs and be part of the family."

"I'm writing."

"Writing what? Come downstairs. Writing alone in your room is unnatural for a girl of your age."

She left my bedroom door wide open, marched downstairs and closed the living room door behind her—a bit too triumphantly. I slid the journal under my pillow, took the stairs one at a time, slipped quietly into the living room. Everyone looked up. Mum, Dad and my four little sisters, their faces glowing blue in the light of the TV. I slumped down between two sisters, onto the plush floral carpet, as Coronation Street started.

That memory crashed into me, up there in the attic on top of Mum's bedroom. I never forgot that word, "unnatural". The way she said it. It sounded bad, dirty even.

I knew Mum was wrong. But part of me believed her. Maybe there was something wrong with me wanting to talk to myself in a notebook, when normal people talked to their friends. Maybe I was unnatural.

Another writing memory comes in a flash. I'm only five or six. My toes don't scrape the floor yet when I swing my legs under the desk. A giant black shadow hovers in front of me, stabbing a chalky fingernail into my blank new notebook.

"Susan Ward. You haven't started yet."

"No Sister."

It's not that it's too hard. It's only a story about the school holidays. I'm just waiting for it to start. Very soon the words will slide from my head, down my arm through my hand and out the end of my pencil. I know, somehow, that's how stories come. If I wait. If I believe. They will just come out the end of the pencil.

"What is your story about?"

"What grass smells like. When Dad cuts it and fills up the big box and we jump in from the gum tree. That smell. Sister."

"You can't write about a *smell,* Susan. Write about something you *did*. And hurry up."

I feel heat creeping up my neck, a tight hot ball stuck in my throat, tingling cheeks and the tiniest prick of tears. Don't let them out. Push back down. Push. Blink hard, swallow hard. Swallow again.

"Yes Sister."

I knew Sister was wrong too. I could so write about a smell. Especially that smell. If I waited. If I remembered hard. *Cool damp soft chopped grass in a giant cardboard box. Climb the gum tree jump in and suck that tangy green hard up your nose through your whole body. Lie still and float. Summer. Dad and his push mower. Hush mower.*

Do what you're told.

I wrote a story about visiting a farm and feeding lambs with a baby's bottle. It was the first of many grammar-perfect, spelling-perfect tidy little good-girl stories that earned me gold stars and English prizes at the end of the school year.

I sat at Dad's desk, closed the journal. I felt hot tickling on my cheeks. Tears. But not for my dying mother. I was crying for that girl, 16 and unnatural.

I didn't want to feel resentful and angry. But that's exactly how I felt. Even frail and dying, Mum still felt like a huge force that could crumple me.

Chapter 4
ONE OF THE GIRLS

The door from the house into the garage opens and smashes into the ladder. I hear a muffled curse, a laugh, creaking on each step. A blonde head pops up out of the floor. It's Julie. The second oldest Ward girl. I'm the oldest.

"Are you hiding up here?"

"Yep."

"Do you want a drink? All the girls are here so we thought we'd open a good bottle of wine."

"I'd love one. Is Father gone?"

"Yep, he just left. Nana's gone too. There are other visitors. Mum's fine."

Julie appears head first from the floor, followed by shoulders, torso, legs all lit from underneath, like one of those lawn decorations, inflating from the ground up.

"What have you found?"

"My old journal from when I was 16. And look, Fat Santa."

"Remember when Mum stuffed him up the chimney at Christmas. Over the Baby-Jesus crib."

"Yeah. I found those plaid pinafores she made us. From years ago."

"Too bad we can't fit them now."

"That would make her happy, seeing us in matching outfits."

"Maybe we could buy matching outfits for the funeral."

"Stop it!"

"We'll have to go through all this stuff at some point."

"Yeah. Not now though. Let's have a drink."

I switched off the bare light bulb and followed Julie down the ladder, closing the trap door after me, the journal tucked under my arm. I slipped into the spare bedroom on the way down the hall, pushed it under the clothes in my suitcase, joined my sisters in the living room.

They had the family photos out. Our family didn't go in much for photo albums. Most of the photos were stuffed into an old cardboard box. Some were labelled. Most weren't.

"Susie, there are so many baby photos of you. I always knew you were the favourite!"

"I was just the first—a bit of a novelty."

"Firstborn. That's what Mum called you."

"That was creepy."

"She was proud of you."

"No she wasn't."

"There are hardly any photos of me."

"Here's one, Maria. I remember that day."

"Man, I was chubby."

"You were a cutie!"

"None of us were pretty babies. We were all quite plain when we were born."

"Julie was a gorgeous baby."

"My head was *huge* when I was born. Look Susie, it's almost as big as yours and you were already three."

"Wow, look at those dresses. Can you believe Mum made us all matching outfits?"

"I hated those dresses."

"Why? We were so fashionable."

"Because I was 11 and I was dressed the same as my one-year-old baby sister. It was so embarrassing."

"Mum loved it when people went gaga over our matching clothes, eh?"

"Haha, look at you Ange. No wonder we called you spaghetti legs!"

"I wish they were that skinny now."

"Awww, Polly, look at your gorgeous curly hair."

"Hey, look at Dad. He's so gorgeous in this photo. How old do you think he is?"

"16? 17? He's gorgeous."

I soaked in my sisters. We weren't together much, with me living overseas.

There's a photo of the five of us at Dad's funeral. Another one taken at Julie's wedding. We don't look particularly alike, but we do look like sisters. At that time, when Mum was dying, I didn't really know my sisters as adults. And they didn't know me. I almost never spoke to them. I'd talk to Mum on the phone, and she'd pass on any news. But when we did get together, it felt easy. We understood each other. We were comfortable together.

Later, without Mum as an intermediary, I got to know each of them much better. They are such warm, kind, funny, talented women. Even if they weren't my sisters, I'd want them to be my friends.

"We should get another photo of us all while you're home, Susie." Maria read my mind.

"Don't worry, we'll get herded up for photos at the funeral."

"Do you think we should all be pall bearers? At the funeral."

"Don't talk about the funeral! Mum's not dead yet."

"She hasn't got long to go."

"How do you know that?"

"The hospice nurse said. This morning."

"What do they know?"

We all look down at the photos in our hands, in piles on the floor. I'm holding six photos fanned out like playing cards. Six photos taken over ten years. These are the sisters I know. In each photo I have a different new baby under my arm. The baby is always dressed in white. The rest of us are in new, identical outfits.

The photographer would come to the house in those days. There would be what felt like hours of ironing, curling, washing, dressing and practicing our best smiles before he arrived. He and Mum would arrange us on a table top or the sofa, where we'd be made to stay perfectly still for far too long. I had two bodies to keep still—my own and the latest baby's. We were under tremendous pressure to be the best looking kids on Earth for those photos. Over the years our easy smiles become anxious grimaces. We're desperately trying to get it right, trying not ruin the photos Mum wants to send to all the relatives for Christmas.

I deal the photos out onto the carpet around my feet. "Look at these. I wonder how many dresses Mum made us over the years."

"Must have been hundreds."

"Look at us playing with our dolls. We were always playing dolls."

"How come you never played dolls with us, Susie? You're in none of these photos."

I knew this was coming. "I was looking after you all. I couldn't play with you and look after you at the same time. I had to make sure nothing bad happened to you."

"Why?"

"Because that was my job. I thought I had to."

"We thought you didn't like us."

"And we thought you were Mum and Dad's favourite."

"I was *not*. I was useful, that's all."

This conversation happened every time we got together. It was good-natured, and we usually had a laugh. But tonight it made me sad. It took me back to a Sunday morning in winter, in the big kitchen in the house on Princes Street, when I was 11, and about to get the shock of my life.

Mum was making tomato soup for the picnic, heating up a can of Wattie's, adding milk and pepper and a dollop of butter. I can see the family-size thermos, a dull grey green, standing on the kitchen counter. Mum stirred the soup in a pot on the stove. Dad leaned against the counter, waiting for the butter to soften in a dish on top of the kettle, so he could spread the thin white Sunday bread for sandwiches.

The girls, all four of them, are a giggly tangle of sweaters and coats and boots. I'm watching from the kitchen table.

There's always chaos around clothes. Mostly because of the matching. Also, Mum never puts labels or even initials on our clothes, and they're all kept in the same cupboard. One sister always ends up with a too-small coat while another's drowning in a too-big one. You have to get everyone to take the coats off, then you need to hold them up, back to back, armpit to armpit, redistribute them, and put them on quick, before they get mixed up again. This is only coats. Imagine the socks and dresses and cardies and pyjamas and underwear. It's a nightmare.

But I'm 11 now, and we just got an automatic washing machine, so I'm allowed to do my own laundry. I keep my own clothes, which I wash and dry and fold and iron myself, in my room. It's heaven. So much better than scrounging for a pair of socks and knickers and a blouse every morning.

I'm dressed and ready to go.

"Come and help the girls get their coats and boots on, Susan. We're nearly ready."

"Alright. I'm coming."

I start by unwinding them, standing them in a row, biggest to littlest. We line up the coats and the boots, each pair of boots in size order with a left and a right. The older two can dress themselves. The little ones need their arms pulled through the coat sleeves so their sweaters don't bunch up to their elbows. They need their zippers done up, a hat pulled over their head, boots checked to see they're on the right feet.

"Susan, make sure their faces are washed before they get in the car."

You have to hold their heads still, and I find cupping my hand under their chin, and making funny faces at them usually gives me enough time to rub whatever breakfast or snot or crumbs lurk around

their mouths and noses. Mum will check, so I have to do it properly.

"Are the girls ready to go, Susan?"

I checked. They were ready. Mum wrestled the thermos into the picnic box.

Dad picked the box up off the counter in both hands. "Come on you girls, hurry up. We're leaving. Susie, Julie, Polly, Maria, Angela. Get into the car you girls, all of you!"

The four girls tumbled towards the back door. I didn't move. I stared at Dad. What did he just say?

"Come on Susie! What's the matter with you?"

"Dad?"

"What?"

"Am I one of the girls?"

Dad laughed his deepest loudest laugh—the one he saved for only the very best jokes.

"Don't be a ninny. Of course you are. Get in the car."

I didn't know. I knew they were my sisters. I knew I wasn't their mother; not exactly. But it had never occurred to me that I was one of *them.*

To say my sense of identity was shattered that day might be over-dramatic. But it was very bad news. Even at 11, I knew there must be something seriously wrong with a girl who didn't know who she was.

I did think looking after the girls was my job. I was going to say "for my whole life", all 11 years of it, but for almost three years, I was an only child. Firstborn, Mum used to call me.

I hated that name. It never sounded affectionate, as you might imagine, or even friendly. Maybe that's what she meant, but she always said it in a tone of voice I found threatening, full of expectation. Being Firstborn felt like a burden, not a privilege. I had other names too, growing up. Dad called me Susie mostly, but often Snoozie because I loved my bed. I was the kid who asked if I was allowed to go to bed early and read. Nana Ward named all her grandchildren after nursery rhyme characters. I was her Queen of Hearts. Nana Baird always called me

Susanna. I loved that name. Susanna sounded exactly like the girl I was born to be—the girl I'd be one day, when I wasn't busy looking after my sisters.

I don't remember much about being an only child. But I do remember when Julie was born. Brothers and sisters of the newborns weren't allowed inside "the Home". That's what we called the imposing white maternity hospital on the corner of Dee Street and Gala Street. After Julie was born, Dad and Nana brought me to stand on the lawn outside one of the maternity home ground-level windows, while Mum stood inside waving and pointing to the white blanket bundled in her arms. I think many Invercargill children met their siblings this way.

I have no memory of being excited or jealous or curious about my new sister. I was preoccupied with the hand I was hiding behind my back. Nana Ward had bandaged my burned fingers—I'd been practicing lighting the matches I found in the drawer under her kitchen table. She told me to hold it behind my back so Mum wouldn't see. "Mums don't need to know everything," she said. Dad played along. Nobody growled at me.

The bandage was gone by the time Mum and Julie got home from the hospital. I came home from Nana Ward's place and learned how to help Mum with the baby.

Mum taught me well. I knew how to feed them—stare at them intently, and open your mouth really wide, never breaking eye contact. They can't help themselves from copying you. Put the spoon of food in their gaping mouth, then shut yours. They will shut theirs, and you gently pull out the spoon. Eventually they catch on, and you have to use more extreme tactics, like playing airplanes with the spoon, zooming it around and around your head and their head, then cruising it in for a landing right in their mouth. Works every time.

I knew how to bathe them. Use your elbow to test the water. If it feels too hot or too cold for your elbow, it's going to be too hot or too cold for the girls. Don't ever, ever take your eyes off them when they're in the bath, because if you do they'll drown. You wouldn't believe how fast that can happen. I knew how to wash them and dry them and get them into their pyjamas, tuck them into bed, put them to sleep with songs and stories. I knew how to change nappies, and how to hold the girls on the toilet seat so they don't fall in. I knew how to make them stop crying, how to feed them with a bottle, and how and when to burp them.

When they got a bit older, I took them to school, made sure they didn't get run over, didn't get beaten up by bullies, and didn't get into cars with strangers. We all travelled to and from school together, and I was in charge. We rode our bikes in single file, me in front, checking right then left then right again before we crossed the intersections. I exaggerated the hand signals so they'd learn how to do it. I got them home safely.

At home, I tried to make sure they stayed in the yard, played nicely, didn't drown in the fish pond, didn't get too dirty, didn't swear or be cheeky. When Mum gave me the word, I herded them up and brought them inside, washed their faces and hands, and got them up into their chairs at the table, sorted out any fights about who's getting what animal on their placemat and whose turn for the favourite fork. (Yes, our family had a favourite fork, and you would not believe the competition for it every damned mealtime!)

As I write this, I have to question it. Did I really have to shoulder all that responsibility? I don't know for sure. I just know that's how it *felt.* I felt it was expected of me. If I had a choice, I didn't know it. I just did it. I loved the girls. And I loved my job looking after them. I was really good at it. I liked being good at something.

Sometimes I fool myself. I wasn't always good at it. I broke Polly's leg once, when I dropped her on the floor. I once brought Julie home with blood spurting out a gash on her head, when I couldn't stop her falling off Mr Hunt's trailer. Both occasions ended in trips to the hospital, for which I blamed myself.

I certainly didn't intend to drop Polly on the floor and break her leg. But she was crying. She was too young to sit up, or crawl. I was sure she wanted to get out of the kitchen and into the living room with Mum and Dad and their friends Tony and Jan. We were visiting them in Gore. They didn't have any children, and we felt exceedingly sorry for them.

"Mum, Polly's crying. Can I carry her in here?"

"I don't think you're big enough."

"Yes I am. I'm almost six. I can do it."

"You'll have to be very careful."

Before they let me pick Polly up and carry her, they thought I should practice. Jan got a baby-sized bag of salt out of her pantry and put it on the floor. I bent down, picked up its dead weight, cradled it in my arms, carried it into the living room, and put it gently on Mum's lap. "There you go. The baby."

"Alright, you can bring Polly in now."

I was half way across the kitchen, Polly gripped safely in my arms, when my socks slipped out from under me, and we crashed to the floor.

Polly had a heavy plaster cast on the broken leg for a few weeks. Dad said it was brilliant because Polly could suddenly sit up without falling over—the weight of the plaster anchored her forward. Mum said it was Jan's fault for having such a shiny kitchen floor. I knew it was my fault.

When Polly got the plaster cast off weeks later, she couldn't sit up any more. Without the extra weight, she kept crashing backwards, banging her head on the floor. I knew that was my fault too.

And here we are, the five Ward girls in our mother's house, going through the photo box, laughing and crying, all adults now. I'm 38, Ange's 28. We don't wear matching clothes any more. Our father is dead. Our mother is dying. How did this all happen?

Later, after the girls left, I fished the journal out of the bottom of my suitcase. You'd never know by reading it that I had four younger sisters. I don't mention them at all. I hardly mention Mum and Dad. There's a cast of high-school characters constantly coming and going. I have my first kiss in the back seat of a car at Oreti Beach. I remember that kiss, a confusing mix of thrill and disappointment, triggering weeks of agony over a boy I was willing to love, but never saw again.

"What are you doing, Susan?"

"Reading an old diary. Are you awake?"

"Hmmm. Did Nana come back?"

"Yes, but you were asleep."

"You should have woken me up! I need to talk to her."

"Then why did you send her away this afternoon? She came as soon as we called her." Mum had unceremoniously dismissed her mother a few hours earlier, after insisting on seeing her. Nana was crying when she left the house.

"How can I talk to her when she's got no batteries in her hearing aids?"

"She went to the hospital and got them fixed. She'll come back tomorrow.

"She might be too late."

Chapter 5
BEST DRESSED

"What are we going to do with all her clothes?"

"I don't know. Give them away?"

My sisters and I talk quietly into Mum's open closet. Mum's sleeping.

"I'll take some of them. She's got some really nice things."

"She said she wants to be buried in her wedding dress."

"The one in the dress-up box? When she married Dad?"

"No, the one she wore when she got married to Michael. This navy one."

"I think she made that dress."

"Does she still sew?"

"Not as much. But sometimes. Someone said she's been hallucinating about sewing."

"Yeah. She's been hand stitching a hem for hours on end."

"She made us so many clothes eh?"

"That's what everyone remembers about the Ward girls. Our matching outfits."

Mum made almost all our clothes. She'd come home from town, thrilled with the yards of fabric and trim, the latest dress pattern. She'd shake out the fabric and drape it around us, seeing the perfect outfits in her mind.

Matching girls—her calling, her life work.

I remember the angry black snippy snip scissors. The whizz-clatter of the Singer sewing machine. The curses. The tears. The beaming smile when it all worked out in the end. All of us standing there in a row, little fashion soldiers.

People would exclaim at the outfits, always fashionable, sometimes edgy but in a modest, proper way. We were the dolls she dressed up and took out to show off—clean, well-behaved, matching.

I can still see Mum, bent over that shiny black sewing machine, steering the tight curves of an underarm or neckline around the speeding needle, like a racing car driver straining to hold it on the road. When Mum sewed, we were in a constant state of siege: strip off, try on, get dressed, strip off. She'd stand up from the sewing machine, wave, talking with her bony beckoning finger, "Come here!", her mouth pinched around a dozen dressmaking pins poking sharp-end-out from between her lips; a ferocious fish mouth.

The half-made dresses, bits still pinned together, stabbed when we moved, even a little bit. Sewing was gruelling. It took over the whole household. But it had to be done. We had to have new outfits. And they had to match.

Every day when we were growing up, Mum told us what to wear. "You're wearing the green dresses with the blue collars today!" she'd announce as we finished breakfast, "Go and get dressed."

"Put on your red shorts and the red and white striped t-shirts, with the blue sneakers and blue and white striped socks."

Everything matched. Not just the fancy, going-out outfits. Our messing about at home clothes matched too. Even our pyjamas, our dressing gowns and slippers.

Dad used to tell the story of looking around the house for some lost building plans. He opened the closet in the spare room, and discovered a whole row of matching baby outfits—dresses, bonnets and bloomer sets—hung on hangers, waiting for the first baby to arrive. Mum was only about five minutes pregnant according to Dad, and she'd already made all those outfits. "It's a good thing you were a girl, Susie!"

It certainly was. I truly believed if I had been born a boy, Mum would have sent me back, and tried again for a daughter she could dress up in those outfits. I suppose I spent my gestation pressed up against a sewing table, absorbing the clatter and whir of a Singer sewing machine.

The clothing rules went like this: Babies wore white or pale pink until they were about a year old. Then they got outfits to match the rest of us. Mum had her last baby in 1970, so the following year she reached the holy grail of motherhood – she got to dress all five of us the same.

She bought yards of bright green cotton, printed with white, orange and hot-pink daisies for the dresses, white crepe polyester for the blouses. The skirts were high-waisted, gathered with shirring elastic, with straps up the front and over the shoulders. The blouses had short puffed sleeves, overstitched on the edges with green, orange, hot-pink. We looked like a scene out of the Sound of Music in those dresses. We wore them everywhere that summer—to Mass every Sunday, to Christmas lunch at Nana's, on our family holiday.

You can't tell from the photos, but the mania for matching outfits was so out of control some of the flowers from the scraps of fabric got cut out and sewn onto Dad's undies. Maybe I did some of the stitching, but it was definitely at Mum's direction. Dad didn't bother protesting.

At 11, the last thing I wanted was to be part of a matching freak show with my sisters aged eight, five, three and one. But too bad for me. I had no say in what I wore. This was Mum's moment. We got so much attention, people ooh-ing and ahh-ing and gushing about how adorable we looked.

I overheard an aunty on Christmas Day saying to Mum, "Susan's not going to want to wear the same clothes as her little sisters for much longer." I honestly don't know if I remember her reply, or if I'm making this up, "Susan will wear what I tell her to." But that's what it felt like.

One year we went on a holiday to visit Dad's family in the North Island. Mum made Julie, Polly and me mustard-coloured skirts with suspender straps over cream blouses especially for that trip. The oversized collars and cuffs had a fancy mustard stitch trim that Mum's new sewing machine miraculously produced at the turn of a dial. And we had brown lace-up knee-length boots. Imitation crocodile. Mum had only found boots to fit Julie and me in Invercargill. There were none in Polly's size.

I remember nothing else about that days-long drive except that Mum got Dad to stop at every Hannah's shoe shop between Gore and Levin to find those boots in Polly's size. None of the shops had them, until Levin, which was so close to our destination it was almost a Total Disaster. But the boots in Polly's size were there at Hannah's on the main street of Levin, just as Mum knew they would be. Now I think about it, she would have bought them too big if that was her only option. But they did fit. We matched. That was all that counted.

Then there were the orange vinyl coats. They were just for Julie and me; we were five and eight. It was bean bag vinyl, stippled to look like leather. The coats were just slightly flared, above-the-knee, identical twins with wide collars and three-quarter length sleeves. Dad hammered the silver snap dome fasteners up the front. Mum hand stitched around the collars and pockets and down the front openings with heavy brown thread. I know she broke more than a few needles on that oversewing.

Those coats were a real statement. They were also heavy and stiff. We could hardly move in them. This didn't bother Mum. She liked her children to stand still and look good. I remember feeling confused in that coat. It's a new coat, it's a happy orange colour. I want to be happy. But I feel like a cardboard cut-out doll. Flat and stiff. I can't run or play. I can just stand there with my arms sticking out so the seams don't poke my armpits.

I feel like I've got white gloves on, but no, that's another outfit, another awkward dressing up moment, standing outside the Sacred Heart Church at a little sister's christening in a powder blue coat. White gloves. Not knowing what to do or say. Or feel. Just being good. Staying clean.

I wished I'd had the guts to yell out, "Hello! There's a human being trapped inside this coat! Let me out!"

I'm surprised that in all the family photos, there are none of us wearing those coats. They were such a dressmaking achievement.

Even school uniforms were a big deal. That's all I can remember about starting school—a red and white quarter-inch gingham dress with short sleeves, buttons down the front to the waist, and a gathered knee-length skirt. Red cardigan, white socks, black knickers, black shoes and a red beret, accessorized with a red school case, red lunch box, and red drink bottle.

I don't remember how many trial runs we had putting on that uniform. Lots. Mum made the dress, so there were many fittings and tuckings, tweakings, and stabbings with pins. There was the final hemming, requiring the wearing of the right shoes, standing on the kitchen table, very still, straight, no hopping or jiggling, turning in super-slow motion as Mum checked the length and made tiny adjustments.

In the weeks before I started school, Mum insisted we model my uniform to everyone who visited. I'd stand in my red gingham dress, shiny new shoes, holding my new case, waiting while Mum fussed with the beret so it was cocked just so. I was mortified because we were told constantly not to show off, yet Mum was always showing us off. I paraded, solemnly, on command, for whoever came to the house, worried about sinning by showing off, but worried much more about sinning by disobeying my mother.

My uniform wasn't quite enough excitement for Mum though. One afternoon soon after I'd started school, I came home on the school bus, and trudged into the house, making a beeline for my room and Squinty, my favourite doll with the scrunched up face. Squinty wasn't allowed to come to school with me. I missed her all day. But she wasn't in my room. I ran down to the kitchen, "Where's Squinty?"

"She's over there!" Mum pointed to the dining table.

Squinty squinted at me from under a red beret. She wore a Sacred Heart School uniform, exactly like mine. She even had a red doll's suitcase tied to her wrist. Mum was so excited. I was thrilled. Matching Squinty was way better than matching my little sisters. Where on earth Mum found the time or energy to make my doll a school uniform I'll never know. She had a new baby and a toddler. But nothing ever stopped her from having everything match.

You can imagine the stress.

Mum's beaming pride in her matching girls, crumpled easily into rage and tears over the laundry chaos, the morning dressing chaos, spills and stains.

When we were going out, to Mass or to town, or visiting, we'd put on the outfits Mum told us to wear, and present ourselves for inspection. If we passed, she or Dad would take off our outer layer—a cardigan or jacket—turn it inside-out, then put it back on us. When we arrived at our destination, last minute before getting out of the car we'd turn our top layer right-side-out, turn our faces to Mum, who had a handkerchief in her hand, ready to spit and wipe off any last specs of dirt. If we had a family crest, it would say: Clean On Arrival.

Clothing chaos was a real problem in our house. At some point Dad decided to solve it by designing an underwear filing system. I think Dad drew it up, and Mum made it—a sheet of fabric with nine pouches sewn onto it, three across and three deep, nailed to the inside of the door to the hot water heater cupboard in the kitchen. The top row was mine, one pouch for undies, one for socks, and one for singlets. Julie had the middle row. Polly had the bottom row.

Dad reasoned that whoever folded the laundry, Mum or me, would simply file the underwear in the correct pouch—a sure-fire end to the insanity. Of course it failed. If Mum or I had known what underwear belonged to what child, there would be no chaos in the first place. But with everything matching, the similar sizes, the determined refusal to label any clothing, the underwear defied sorting. Why didn't we label? It would have solved so much. I thought it was because only poor people labelled their children's clothing. We didn't want any signs of poverty.

I worked the system, filing the cleanest, newest items in my own pouches—the socks with the thickest soles, the underwear with still-stretchy elastic. Anything with holes, slack elastic went into Julie's or Polly's pouches. They caught on. We agreed to use the middle row for undies, the bottom row for socks, the top row for singlets. We slipped back to the first-up-best-dressed system, along with its fights and tears.

Mum didn't talk much about her childhood, but when she did, it didn't sound like it was a happy one. She told us that because she and her sisters didn't have the correct school uniform in high school, the nuns made them walk at the back of the line to Mass. She felt poor. Humiliated. Less than.

She told us that she always had hand-me-down clothes and toys. Even her underwear was second hand from her sisters or cousins. Sometimes Nana would stay up all night sewing. In the morning there would be three new dresses hanging from the drying rack in the kitchen. But they were made from old fabrics, from someone else's old clothes.

I suppose it's not surprising she was obsessed about dressing us up. Maybe she was just trying to protect us from suffering the humiliation she suffered as a girl. Maybe. It seemed to me she always took it a bit too far.

"Aunty Susie! We're trying on the wedding dresses. It's your turn." My nieces were up in Mum's room, rummaging in the closet. Mum lay still. Eyes closed. She wouldn't be playing this time.

The wedding dress game. Every time I came home we played it. There were three wedding dresses in the dress-up box. Nana's, a straight floor-length satin sheath from the mid-1930s. Nana must have been a waif when she got married. Mum's from 1959, fitted top, tiny wasp waist, long lace sleeves, extravagant flared calf-length skirt. And mine, from 1983. Long-sleeved, high-necked, ruffled and bowed. The marriage was over, but the dress survived.

You win if you can fit into them all. Including doing up all the buttons and zips. I know I can fit into mine still, and probably Mum's. I'm kind of scrawny at the moment. But I don't remember when I last fit into Nana's. Years ago.

"Try it, Aunty Susie."

I pulled off my track pants and sweat shirt, and slid the cool smooth satin over my head. It slithered over my shoulders, belly and hips, puddled around my feet. It was so cool, simple, luxurious.

"Can someone do up the buttons?"

"Hold your tummy in."

It wasn't going to happen.

"Put on the next one." Mum's wedding dress is a 1950s classic. I suck in again, and my nieces can do up the buttons. I take a twirl. The calf length super full skirt flutters out and falls into perfect folds. Mum looked gorgeous on her wedding day in this dress. It was a July wedding. Winter. Her bridesmaid and flower girl, Mum's older sister Patricia and her baby sister Joanne, wore red velvet.

Dad looks dapper in his suit. But many times he told us how uncomfortable he was that day, not able to take off his suit jacket because the trousers he picked up from the suit rental shop on the morning of the wedding were about ten times too big, and he had to safety-pin the waistband to the underarms of his shirt so they wouldn't fall down around his ankles. "The guy who measured my leg length must have stuck his ruler right up my arse," he'd laugh.

"Put on your old wedding dress, Aunty Susie."

I don't want to, but I put it on. It's still scratchy. After all these years I still hate it.

"This was meant to be a silk dress."

Silk. The colour of milk with a drop of cocoa. It rustled when it moved, made a kind of silky shudder when I shook it out in front of me, kicked it gently with my bare foot.

I bought the whole roll, and had it sent to the dressmaker. When she rang to say it was time for the first fitting, Mum was excited. "Why don't we make a day of it? We can drive up to Gore to pick up Faye, then we'll all go to Pat's for the fitting." *Too excited.*

"Faye probably doesn't want to go to the dress fitting, Mum. It's just for sizing. It won't even look like a wedding dress yet."

"She does want to come. I talked to her yesterday. We're picking her up at 10. Pat's expecting us all."

"But Mum..."

"Don't argue. We both want to see the dress."

It seemed odd that Mum and my future mother-in-law would plan to come to this fitting. And I really didn't want them there. I didn't want anyone interfering with this dress. God knows they'd interfered with everything else.

When I showed her a sample of the silk I'd bought, Mum bristled. "Silk! That's a terrible fabric for a wedding dress."

"It's beautiful, Mum. You didn't want me to have muslin, so I picked silk. I love it. Princess Diana had silk just like this and it looked amazing!"

"I told you silk will crush the minute you sit down on it. If it's a warm day it will wilt and you'll look like you're wearing a dish rag! I can't believe you bought silk."

Well, I did buy silk. I spent every penny I had on that silk.

I'd also picked the pattern, playing it safe with a full long skirt and long sleeves just like Princess Diana's, but with a higher neckline.

"That's not very feminine."

I wanted to forage for wild lupins for my bouquet. I'd get up early on the wedding day, go to Oreti Beach for a long barefoot walk, and pick the lupins from the roadside on the way back. The tall dark purple ones.

"Nola will do your bouquet. She makes beautiful flower arrangements. We'll get the flowers from Mrs Phillips. Her mock orange will be in bud right on time. We'll have a basket, so the flowers stay looking nice all day."

I planned to wear just the barest hint of lipstick. No pretentious bridal makeup. And I wasn't wearing heels.

"Why do you always want to be so unladylike, Susan? You can't wear flat shoes and no makeup to your own wedding!"

We picked Faye up at 10, and drove to Pat's. Her sewing room was dingy. Why did she have the lights off? She herded us inside, and as my eyes adjusted to the dark, I saw a ghost of a dress hanging from a hook on the wall opposite. Like the bride had evaporated out of it.

Pat switched on the light.

"Whose dress is that?" I asked, pointing to the ghost.

"It's yours!"

"But it's the wrong material. It's a different colour." I could see that from across the room. I walked over, close enough now to touch it and feel it was cheap and prickly. It wasn't my silk. Did the shop ship the wrong material? Did Pat mix my fabric up with someone else's? What had gone wrong? I was scrambling to make sense of what had happened. Mum, Faye and Pat all started talking at once.

"Yes it is your dress. No, it's not the silk you bought. When Pat unrolled it, it had a flaw. We decided to send it back and get something else, almost exactly the same. It's a very close colour. It really looks like silk, but it's Polyester, so it won't wilt or crush. Nobody will know but us. It's going to be beautiful."

"It had a flaw? But I unrolled it in the shop and it was fine. It didn't have a flaw."

"It did have a flaw. Silk often does."

I knew it didn't have a flaw. "Why didn't you tell me?"

"We didn't want to upset you so close to the wedding, so we all talked, and decided to get a new fabric. We found one almost identical. It's going to be perfect. Try it on."

I felt myself shrinking, sucking in and up. Sometimes when I'm outraged I kind of vaporize out of my body and hover overhead, out of harm's way. I can see but not feel what's happening. Nobody else notices. I just watch myself, in silence, do what has to be done. It might be a few minutes or hours before I come back.

I watched myself put on the ghost dress. Yellowish, scratchy. The high neck was too high. There were no sleeves in it yet. It annoyed my armpits. They poked and prodded; Pat pinned and tucked. I twirled on command.

"Great, we'll have another fitting in a week, and it will be finished in plenty of time for the wedding." Pat seemed happy.

We had tea and scones in Pat's kitchen. We got in the car. I wasn't back in my body yet. I was still registering what just happened. *They changed my dress fabric without telling me? My wedding dress is polyester?* If WTF was a thing in those days, I would have been, *seriously WTF?*

I sat in the back of Mum's green Fiat. Mum and Faye chatted in the front as we drove North to Gore. We stopped outside my parents-in-law's place while Faye got out, and I got in the front passenger seat. Mum and I took off down Highway 1 to Invercargill. Mum at the wheel, chattering on about the lucky save, isn't Pat great to be making this dress for your wedding gift, it was nice that Faye could come along. Me staring out at blips of purple lupins on the roadside. I don't know if I said anything.

I went to the next fitting by myself. The dress fit fine, and it had sleeves, but it was still scratchy and still yellow. And it was too long.

"I won't be wearing heels, Pat, so would you please shorten the hem a couple of inches?"

A week before the wedding, the dress arrived in a huge box in the back of my fiancé's car.

"Do you want to see it?" I asked.

"That's bad luck isn't it?"

"This dress has been nothing but bad luck. I don't think it could get any worse."

"I think I can wait a week."

Mum couldn't wait a minute. "Put it on and let me have a look!"

I put it on. I wasn't happy.

"Dammit. I asked Pat to take it up two inches. It's still far too long!"

"Oh dear. She must have forgotten. Well we can't ask Pat to do any more work on it now. We'll just have to get some shoes with a decent heel, and it will be perfect."

The polyester scratched again as I pulled the wedding dress off and stuffed it back in the dress-up box.

"I need to have a shower," I muttered, and strode down the hall in my underwear into the bathroom. Locked myself in. Turned the shower taps on full. Undressed. Glanced in the mirror and scowled.

Why did I let her get away with that? Why didn't I say something?

Paralyzed. Still am.

The hot tears on my face melted into the hot blast of the shower water.

Chapter 6
LOOKING GOOD

"Can I look in the mirror?"

"I don't think you want to do that, Mum. You're not looking that flash."

"I want to see."

"Put your teeth in first."

Her teeth had been hurting her mouth; we'd put them in a glass of water on her bedside table.

I held the glass while she fished them out and struggled to get them into her mouth.

"Better?" she tried to smile. She'd forgotten about the mirror already. I was grateful. She'd aged 20 years in the past few days.

"I remember the day you had all your teeth taken out."

"Do you? You'd be too young to remember that."

"I was three. And I do remember it. I think it's my first memory of you."

I definitely remember the day she had all her teeth pulled out. Every last one of them. It was 1963;

dentures were the rage. Mum was 24 years old. I was three. She left me with Nana, her mother, while she went to town for the afternoon. When she came back, she wasn't my beautiful mother any more. Her face was caved in and bruised, her mouth was an ugly red gash with no lips. She lay down in Nana's bed. I crawled into the baby bed next to hers, my back to my smashed up mother.

"Susan. Are you there? Let me see you."

I rolled over, head still under the blanket. "Is your mouth looking?" I don't remember saying that, but Mum told me that's what I'd said.

"No, it's not looking."

Slowly I pulled the blanket off my head and peeped. Her caved in mouth was shut tight. Then it flashed open, red and sore. She laughed; I screamed and ducked under the covers again.

"Is your mouth looking now?"

"No. Not now."

And so I got used to Mum with no teeth. Then a few weeks later she came back from town looking like her old self again. Her mouth no longer sucked into her head, lipless. She looked normal. Until she smiled, flashing her perfectly straight pearly white new teeth.

Mum really had a thing about teeth. When I was eight or nine, she decided there was something wrong with my teeth. They were crowded. The eye teeth stuck out. She booked me in to a real dentist to see about getting them fixed.

"Big smile so I can have a good look."

I cheesy grin at the dentist, glance at Mum, to make sure I'm doing it right. She nods OK.

I keep grinning at Mr Chin. A man dentist, not a dental nurse. He's Chinese. My Dad's dentist. He comes close and stares at my teeth, from the front, from the sides. I stare at his eyes. I can't believe I can get this close to someone who's Chinese.

I couldn't care less about how my teeth look. But I like the attention. Mum taking me out of school, driving me to a real appointment. There are no sisters around to herd and watch. Just me and Mum. And Mr Chin. They are taking me seriously. Looking, paying attention. Like I'm important.

"You can close your mouth now, Susan."

"What about those eye teeth, Mr Chin?"

"Well, they do have character!"

"But they're so prominent. Too prominent."

"Braces could push them back in the mouth. We wouldn't need to remove any teeth. She's young enough."

"That sounds great! Susan, your eye teeth could get fixed with braces."

My eye teeth have superpowers. They're razor sharp and can nip through anything, even thick rope, one strand at a time. And they're so long I can hook them over my lower lip for an instant vampire look.

"She'd need to wear them for a year or more."

"That's no trouble at all!"

Mr Chin and Mum talk while I look at the posters of rotting teeth, perfect teeth.

On the way back to school, Mum's staring hard through the car window, driving fast, her chin jutting out, slightly off centre. It's her face when things aren't going her way. And my teeth aren't going her way right now. She can't believe braces could be that expensive.

Later, when Dad gets home, I make vampires while Mum cries telling him how much braces are going to cost.

"Stop that, Susan! You'll ruin your looks. We're trying to fix those teeth, and it's going to cost a fortune!"

There's nothing wrong with my teeth, I think, but don't dare say it.

"There's nothing wrong with her teeth, Rosie."

A few weeks later Mum takes me out of school again and we go back to see Mr Chin. He and Mum have got it all arranged, and Dad has agreed. We're going to pull out the molar directly behind each eye tooth, and I'm going to press on my eye teeth with my thumb and fingers, to push them back in my mouth.

"It's not ideal. But it's a lot cheaper than braces. Ready?" Mr Chin winks at me and jabs a needle into my gum. My face goes numb.

Mum's happy on the way home this time, chatting and laughing. My mouth is full of bloody cotton wads and I can taste that nasty metal blood flavour. It makes me gag. The numbing is wearing off.

"I won't be a vampire any more," I whisper, my mouth full of blood.

"Don't be ridiculous. You're going to look beautiful with those straight teeth. You have to remember to press on them though or you'll have ugly gaps in your mouth."

At home we practice. I use my right hand, the thumb on the right eye tooth, the forefinger on the left eye tooth. Elbow on the table. Then drop the weight of my head forward. A head is surprisingly heavy. Eight-year-old teeth are surprisingly flexible.

"You've got to do this whenever you can Susan. At school when you're sitting at your desk, when you're watching TV, when you're saying your prayers, at Mass. Do it all the time and soon those gaps will be gone and you'll have beautiful teeth."

At school the nuns keep telling me to get my filthy hands out of my mouth before I catch a dreadful disease. Mum comes to school to tell them it's dentist's orders.

Slowly, as I leaned, my front teeth shifted, and the gap left by the two extracted molars closed up. By the time I was ten I was no longer a vampire. Mum was thrilled with how my teeth were fixed, so well and so cheap.

I didn't know it then, but Mum once had prominent front teeth. Buck teeth, she'd say. She was ashamed of them, and she was stuck with them. Nobody got cosmetic dental work in small town New Zealand in the 1940s. Her smile, in all the black and white photos, even her wedding photos, is practiced, revealing just enough of her teeth, but not too much. After she got her perfect dentures, she smiled much bigger for the camera. She wasn't afraid to beam.

Years later, when she needed replacement dentures, she came home from the dentist frustrated and annoyed that they'd made her new set exactly like the old ones.

"I don't want them to look so straight and perfect. They look like false teeth!"

The dentist tried filing and reshaping, staining the bright white out of them, but still Mum wasn't happy.

She asked me if I could get off work for a couple of hours. Come to the dentist with her. I wasn't exactly sure why, but I said yes. I met her at Mr Chin's clinic.

"You remember Susan? You took out two of her molars so her eye teeth would drop back."

"Ah yes, instead of braces. How long ago was that now?"

"Ten years."

"Let's see how they look."

I smiled.

"Good. Very good. They look very natural."

"That's what I want my teeth to look like, Mr Chin. Exactly like Susan's."

Our hair was another problem. Not Polly's hair—she had gorgeous natural curls. But Julie and I had straight hair. Julie's at least was blonde. Mine was plain old straight brown—brunette if you were being really generous.

"In the olden days," Mum lectured, "all girls had rags in their hair when they went to bed, so they'd have beautiful ringlets in the morning." She ripped up old sheets into long thin strips, wet them under the tap, wound clumps of our hair around them, the bound them up with more and more rags until thick white bandages the size of sausages poked out the sides of our heads.

Our hair hurt at the roots; the lumpy bandages stuck into our heads. We couldn't sleep. We didn't want stupid ringlets.

"You're going to have to put up with *some* pain for beauty!"

But no matter how tight the rags, how long we left them in, our ringlets would only hold for half an hour before they went lanky. We were jealous of Polly, with her thick natural curls. She didn't need rags.

Mum decided we'd get naturally glowing hair, and maybe even curls, if we all got 100 strokes of the hairbrush every night before bed. She made us sit at her feet in front of her armchair and count each vigorous stroke.

One hundred strokes of the hairbrush ran its course too. We got home perms. All flops. Mum gave up and sent Julie and me around the corner to the hair dresser after making us memorise the instructions, "Please cut it short and tapered." I think we said, "short and tepid" but never mind. We'd failed.

Polly's long curly mane was Mum's pride and joy. Polly hated it. She wanted short hair like her big sisters. Mum would not cut it.

We'd been visiting at Aunty Pat and Uncle Jim O'Brien's for several hours on a Saturday night. The adults were fuzzy with their drinks. They'd stopped sending us outside to play, and we'd settled into the kitchen to listen to Dad and Jim talk and laugh. Polly's hair was bothering her, as usual. She whined again and again that she wanted it cut.

It happened so fast, but in such slow motion, I can still see it as if frame by frame.

Dad turns to Jim.

"Where are your scissors, Jim?"

Jim pulls open a kitchen drawer and points. Dad reaches in and pulls out a big pair of metal scissors.

"Come here Polly. Are you sure you want short hair?"

She nods, very seriously. Her eyes are huge.

He reaches down, picks up a long pigtail off her left shoulder and cuts it off, right on top of the elastic band.

"Go and ask your mother what side she likes the best!" He roars laughing.

We are all speechless.

Polly, only five years old, eyes still huge, walks, grinning uneasily, into the next room, to ask Mum what side she likes best.

And now the memories are a bit fuzzy. I remember our car screaming through the black streets towards home, Mum howling with rage, Dad not saying anything. We kids are a tumble of arms and legs in the back seat, pretending we're sound asleep, but we're electrified.

Mum wouldn't sleep with Dad in their bed. She spent the night on the sofa downstairs. She wouldn't go to Mass with us next morning. She wouldn't speak to Dad, or to any of us for the whole of Sunday. It was as terrifying as it was thrilling. Dad had defied Mum.

Mum went to the 5pm Mass at St Theresa's. The Sign of Peace ritual, where you turn to your neighbours in the pews and say, "Peace be with you", broke the angry spell. Mum turned with her hand extended. The woman beside her looked down, put her hand in Mum's, then looked up. She was grotesque with burn scars. Polly's severed pigtail suddenly seemed like not such a big deal.

Mum smiled at us all when she got home, gave Dad a hug, and got out her dressmaking scissors to straighten Polly's new hairdo.

I've let my hair go grey. It's cropped short.

"You could rinse your hair blonde like mine," almost pleading, while I was trying to straighten up her pillows.

"I like it grey, Mum. I want it to be natural."

"You're too young to be grey."

"I'm grey, Mum. That's what my hair is like. Dad went grey early too, remember."

"Grey looks distinguished on a man."

Chapter 7
MORAL DILEMMAS

The more I write, the more I remember, the more I write.

I question it all—the clothes, the teeth, the hair, the babies, the sewing, the chaos that was our growing up. Was it really that intense? The photo box is full of evidence. Shot after shot of perfectly clean, matching kids, me with a baby perched on my child-sized hip.

Something changed though. On my 12th birthday we had the usual opening of presents in the kitchen at the breakfast table. I don't remember what presents I was given, but I do remember, as I was taking them upstairs to my room, Mum stopping me, saying, "Susan, come with me into the living room for a moment."

She opened the door, and I went in ahead of her. Hanging from a snib on the big sash window, was a long dress. I went closer. It was blue and white one-inch gingham, a floor-length skirt cut on the bias.

A bib with ruffled shoulder straps crossed over the back and buttoned to the waist band. A ruffle floated around the hem. I looked back at Mum. Was it mine? Could it be?

"Happy birthday!" Mum's sing-song voice.

The dress was stylish, perfect. But I loved it most because it was the only one like it in the house—finally I had my own dress, and nobody matched me.

In all the family photos from age 12, I am dressed differently from my sisters, and my hair style is different. I only occasionally have a baby on my hip. I still wore what I was told. Mum still sewed for me. She chose the fabric and the patterns. She also taught me to sew around this time. I started to make my own clothes—from fabric and patterns she approved.

It was a relief, not dressing like my sisters. I felt like I was becoming someone. I wasn't sure who. But it was a hopeful feeling. Things were changing. Mum didn't seem to need me in the same way. She encouraged me to invite school friends over on the weekends. She let me go away on holiday with my friend's family.

Don't think the chains were off. They weren't. But there was a shift.

I stopped doing the practical chores—watching, dressing, feeding, cleaning the girls. My new job was much less practical, but more serious: be a good example to the girls. It was a little bewildering.

It had mostly to do with boys. Which seemed odd, given there were no boys in our family, no boys in my class, and we had very little contact with boys. We'd always known there was something wrong with boys—we knew for sure they were second-rate children. When anyone in the extended family had a baby boy, we felt sorry for that family, their mother in particular. Only girl babies were cause for celebration.

When a boy baby came to our house, Mum went to great lengths to make sure we didn't see their "private parts". But once or twice I saw that tiny pink thing between their legs.

It seems odd to write this, but I knew, or felt I knew that it was impossible for my mother to have boy babies, and I believed this was a great blessing. She was special because she could only have girls.

I didn't know what a miscarriage was, but I did know, from scraps of overheard conversation, that Mum sometimes "lost" a baby—it came out with some blood before it was ready to be born—and when this happened it was just the boys being rejected. I know; it's creepy. But that's what I understood at age 11 or 12.

There was a lot I couldn't get my head around.

"You're the oldest, Susan, so you have to be an example to your sisters. You mustn't get into trouble with boys."

"What boys, Mum?"

"All boys. If you get in trouble with boys, your sisters will all get in trouble too, and it will be your fault. So you need to be very careful."

"Umm. OK?"

"Don't ever tempt boys, Susan.

"Don't dress in a way that could tempt boys.

"Don't go anywhere you might tempt boys.

"If a boy and a girl get in trouble, it is always the girl's fault. Always. The girl can always stop it."

Stop what? I didn't bother asking Mum. I'd cut back on the questions after we had the "girls must have morals" talk. She didn't make much sense.

"Don't forget, Susan, it's very important for girls to have good morals."

"What are morals, Mum?"

"Morals! You know, right and wrong!"

"But what does it mean?"

"Well. If you saw Mum and Dad in the bath—having a bath together—that would be OK, that would be good morals because we are married, right?"

"Umm? Yep?" Our bath was too small for Mum and Dad to fit in it.

"But if you saw Aunty Joanne in the bath with one of her boyfriends, that would be wrong. That would be bad morals. Because they aren't married yet."

"Oh." Aunty Joanne was small enough to fit though.

"Now, it's time for dinner. Go and get the girls inside and wash their hands."

It was bewildering. But I didn't use the bathtub anymore because I was old enough to take a shower, so I figured my morals would be fine.

Barbie dolls were immoral. Because of their large breasts. We didn't call them breasts back then. Titty bottles was the preferred term. For feeding babies. But I'm not writing that phrase more than once. Let's just call them breasts.

Barbie had breasts; therefore she was banned from our house. And if we encountered Barbie at someone else's house, we were expected to look away. Definitely don't play with her. Baby dolls and little girl dolls were the only moral dolls. We had lots of them.

Playing dolls was about the only thing Mum ever wanted us to do. Our dolls had boxes of clothes and nappies, push chairs, high chairs, rattles, bottles, bathtubs. Some dolls even had their own dolls. We washed and fed and dressed and changed dolls all day long. Unless there was a real baby to wash and feed and dress and change.

Other games? Yes, but subject to the strict moral code.

Shops: moral.

Doctors and nurses: immoral.

Playing in sandpit: moral.

Colouring in: moral.

Handstands and cartwheels: moral if you're wearing shorts; immoral if you're wearing a dress.

Communion: moral.

Aunty Joanne: could go either way. Exercise discretion, don't get in the bath with a boyfriend.

Yes, we used to play Communion and Aunty Joanne. Communion required the cutting up of tiny rounds of white bread. We would hold a piece of bread up and pronounce, "Body of Christ" before sitting it reverently on the tongue of our sister who knelt before us. This was a serious game. You weren't allowed to clown around playing Communion.

Aunty Joanne was a little more fun. One of us would be our Aunty Joanne. To play her, you'd act cool. She was seven years older than me, therefore entirely exotic. It seemed she wasn't subject to any rules at all, and we loved to pretend we were her, without a care in the world. And bonus: she had boyfriends. In our games we never tempted the boyfriend of course. Perhaps we'd have a tiff, and run down the driveway in a frenzy pretending we were driving off in a car. Then we'd make up, hold hands. But that was all. Anything else would be immoral.

Tempting boys was puzzling though. When Mum talked about that, I nodded gravely. I took note of the injustice of it always being the girl's fault. Whatever "it" was.

I came to understand that to avoid tempting boys I needed to dress modestly (no bikinis), always be lady-like, never swear or smoke, cross my ankles when I was sitting on a chair, and never go anywhere alone with a boy. Never. If I didn't follow these rules, I'd tempt boys and it would be all my fault. And my sisters would all get into trouble and the whole thing would be a Total Disaster.

There was one rather glaring problem with all of this: Mum was a relentless flirt. She flirted with young men, old men, Dad, the priests, family friends, neighbours, relatives, strangers—even her daughters' boyfriends, later on, when we had them. She'd say provocative and outrageous things. She'd be coy and coquettish, then blush and duck her head as if in shame. She made a sport of tempting boys. It was totally mortifying.

Her flirting backfired on her at least once. Stan and Shirley lived in the house behind ours. They weren't Catholics, but they were good sorts (read: they were drinkers), so it was OK for us to be friends with them. We were such good friends there was a ladder on each side of the huge brick fence between our yards, so we could pop over to visit, babysit, or pick up more beer, instead of walking around the block.

One night at a barbeque in our back yard, Mum flirted with Stan as usual, in front of everyone. I remember her, no doubt fuelled with sweet white wine, wiggling her shoulders, saying something like

"Any time you want Stan, just pop around and see me. I'll be waiting for you."

Stan showed up at the front door on his lunch break one day the following week, when Mum was home alone. We heard the story in snatched bits and pieces of dramatic retelling. Stan came to the door and said, "How about it then, Rosie?" Mum shrieked and slammed the door in his face. The ladder on our side of the fence came down. I wasn't Stan and Shirley's babysitter any more. That's the problem with non-Catholics. They haven't got morals. And they can't take a joke.

Why wasn't it Mum's fault for tempting Stan? An obvious question I didn't dare ask. Even more serious than tempting boys was questioning your mother. Mum did what she liked, and we did what she told us to. Even if they were complete opposites.

I thought Mum was a terrible example to the girls, so I took the job even more seriously. I had morals, I never tempted boys, I never flirted. I hardly spoke to anyone. I minded my own business and wrote in my journal when I needed to say anything important.

Alongside her rampant flirting, Mum's prudishness was legendary. Mum and Dad bought the big old house on Princes Street from Mrs Petrie, widow of artist Jon Petrie. He had doodled over the years on the wallpaper. He left a dizzyingly tall landscape in the stairwell. And he'd painted a frieze around what would be our family room, an enchanting woodland panorama, complete with nubile nymphs. Naked, as nymphs are meant to be.

Before we moved into the house, Mum used white house paint and one of Dad's old paint brushes to paint dresses on them all. I remember the shocked exclamations of family friends when they saw her vandalism. She was utterly unrepentant. She couldn't have naked bodies dancing shamelessly around her living room. What a terrible example for her girls!

In my early teens, Mum kept saying I was a "late developer". She said this to me and to other people, "You're a late developer, aren't you Susan?" She made it sound like being a late developer was an achievement. Like she was glad I was small and flat-chested, that I didn't have my period yet, that I still looked like a kid—that I didn't have what it took to tempt boys.

Puberty happens though, whether your mother likes it or not. I remember a day when I was maybe 13. I was drying myself after taking a shower. The sun must have been setting. A rosy gold light shone through the west-facing bathroom window, a sun beam; a spotlight shining right on my pubis to be precise. And there, in that sunbeam, I saw for the first time, the faintest hint of hair. Golden, downy hair. I don't know how I knew this was about me growing up. But I did know that. I also knew not to tell anyone. Especially not Mum. I knew it was special. *Don't ruin it.*

I talked myself into seeing breasts develop on my flat chest. There were no breasts there. None at all. Maybe if I had a bra, they would grow quicker. Many of the girls in my class wore a bra by then. There was something called a "trainer bra". I imagined they somehow coaxed the breasts out of flat chested girls, miraculously turning us into women.

At 14, not having a bra became an embarrassment, particularly at school. Our day-to-day school uniform covered us up so nobody could see what we had, or didn't have, under our cream cotton shirts. But on gym and swimming days, when the pinafores came off, it was clear who had a bra and who didn't.

Some time during our fourth form year, our class developed a system to relieve the humiliation. The girls who had bras brought their spares to school and lent them to those of us who didn't. We'd slip them on in the toilets, before gym or swimming. We'd be seen with them when it counted, through our blouses, in the change rooms. We'd slip them off and return them to their owners at the end of the school day.

I don't know how often this happened, but I do remember being grateful for this kindness. It *was* a kindness. We all knew the humiliation of being left out, not fitting in.

I wouldn't ask Mum for a bra. You might think that would have been sensible. But trust me, no. It was very important not to let Mum know you wanted anything, particularly if you wanted it badly. Mum would turn it into a high-stakes drama. I'd learned this lesson over a pair sandals.

It was love at first sight when I saw them in the window of Hannah's in early Spring.

"They're golden-orange leather, with a cool pattern stamped into them. They're toe sandals, Mum."

"What's a toe sandal? That sounds odd."

"They have a loop where your big toe goes through. It's a bit like a jandal, but way cooler."

"How much are they?"

"16 dollars."

"16 dollars! We can't afford 16 dollars for one pair of sandals. There are five of you girls to feed and clothe. Imagine if everyone wanted 16-dollar sandals."

"Could I just try them on?"

"We might have a look next time we're in town."

"They might be sold by then."

"We're not buying them anyway, so it won't make any difference."

I tried them on. They fit. Perfectly. I walked proudly around the shop in them, imagining they were mine. But I couldn't have them. They were far too expensive. I already had a pair of perfectly good sandals. There were four other kids in the family who needed shoes too. I understood all that.

A month later, Mum asked what I wanted for my birthday.

"Could I please get the toe sandals?"

"We're not made of money, Susan! But we'll go and see if the shop still has them."

We went to town. They still had the sandals, but my size was all sold out.

"I could get the too-big size. I think my feet are still growing!"

"Don't be ridiculous!"

My birthday came and went. I forget what I got for a present. I was still in love with the toe sandals.

"Maybe we could ask at the shop and see if they could order my size for Christmas."

"Susan thinks we've got enough money to spend 16 dollars on one pair of sandals! She must think we're made of money!"

"What if I got a job and paid for them myself."

"A job doing what?"

"Babysitting? Working in a shop?"

"You're too young to get a job. And you're not to charge for babysitting. You'll do that for free. People aren't made of money you know."

Six weeks later, on Christmas morning, I unwrapped a present, puzzling about what could be inside such an odd-shaped package. Sure enough it was the toe sandals. In my size. Perfect in every way. I was thrilled. Mum was even more thrilled that she'd bought them in Spring, and kept them a secret all this time, putting me off the scent and now giving me such a great surprise for Christmas.

That's why I didn't advertise my longing for a bra. But I might as well have.

Mum came home from a visit with her sister in Christchurch on the Southerner train. Dad picked her up from the station while we girls did the dinner dishes and tidied the kitchen so it looked like things hadn't fallen apart while she was away.

We all gathered around her chair by the fireplace as she sat down, kicked off her shoes, and started rummaging around in a carry bag.

"Here's a present for Dad. And here's one for you, Maria. And Angie. This is for you, Polly. Julie, this is for you. And this is for Susan."

She handed me a small package wrapped in white tissue paper. It was almost weightless. I watched my sisters open their t-shirts, their felt pens, Dad his new socks.

"Open yours, Susan."

I picked open the cellotape, trying not to rip the featherlight paper. Through the first layer I could see a pinky-peach pattern, flowers on a white background. I removed the last layer of tissue, started to unfold the soft silky fabric, then realised what I was holding in my hands. I pushed it back into the tissue paper, eyes pinned to the floor.

"Open it, Susan!"

"But..."

"Open it. Let me see. Do you like it?"

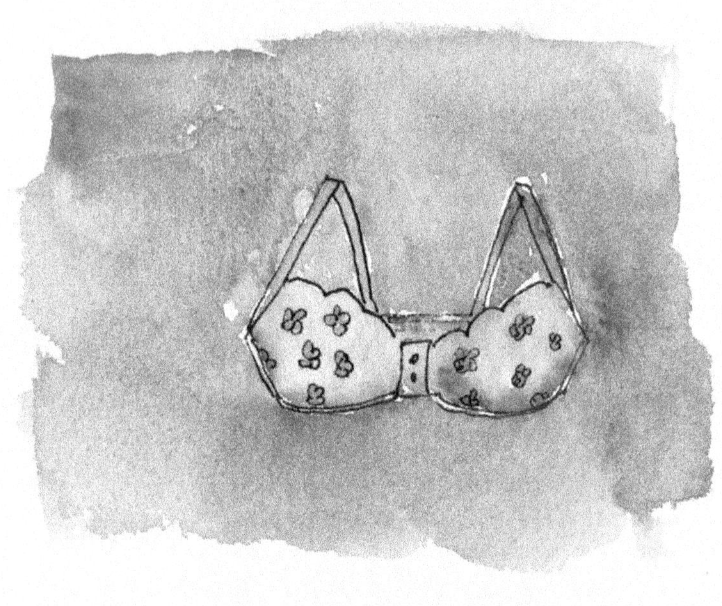

I opened it again, slowly. It was the most beautiful bra I'd ever seen. Much nicer than any of the bras the girls at school wore or lent out. It was plush and pretty and perfect.

"What is it?" A little sister squealed.

"Nothing." I winced.

"It's a beautiful bra I got for Susan in Christchurch!" Mum was so pleased. "Now go and try it on. It might not fit, and we'll have to send it back!"

I climbed the stairs to my room. I took off my school blouse and tried the bra on. It fastened at the front. It fit perfectly—size AA. I looked at myself in the mirror, thrilled. I didn't look like a kid in that bra.

At this point I have what I've come to think of as a split memory. This story has two endings, at least in my mind. I don't know which one actually happened.

In one memory, I'm admiring my new bra in the mirror and Mum knocks gently on my door and lets herself in. She checks the fit and tells me it looks perfect, and I smile at her, put my school blouse on and we go back downstairs together, with a small but important secret between us.

In the other memory, I admire my new bra in the mirror, put my school blouse on and go back downstairs. Mum pounces.

"Let me see!"

I cringed away.

"Lift up your blouse and let me see the fit!"

"Mum! Everyone's looking." I hissed.

"Let me see it," she persisted.

I worried if I didn't do what she wanted, she'd take the bra back and I'd never get another one.

I turned towards her and undid the buttons on my blouse, just low enough that she could see the bra, could see that it fit. Then I did the buttons up quickly, so nobody else would see.

Eventually I got my period. What a relief. I was almost 16.

The tiny bit of blood came overnight, staining my pyjamas the faintest orange brown. Just a smear. I must have told Mum. She must have given me sanitary pads. I know I didn't buy them myself.

I read the instructions on the sanitary pad package. Back then they were thick slabs of papery wadding, pinned onto a cloth belt you wore around your waist. The belt and the pads were way too big for a slim girl-almost-woman. There was no way I could walk normally with that bulk between my legs, no way I could sit on my bike seat. I rode my bike to school standing up.

The instructions said *Incinerate after use*. I knew what incinerate meant, but I looked it up to be sure. *Burn to ashes* declared the battered Oxford Dictionary, with its missing jacket and cracked spine. I was the kind of girl who followed instructions. I'll have to burn them.

Dad had a rusty old 44-gallon drum at the bottom of the garden where he burned yard waste and rubbish. That was the closest thing we had to an incinerator, so the morning after the day I got my first period, I took my first sanitary pads and a box of matches out to the drum, and got busy incinerating.

Have you ever tried to light a sanitary pad on fire? How about a used one? I'm standing over that rusty old drum at the bottom of the garden, lighting match after match after match, and the damned flame would catch for the briefest flash, then extinguish in disgust. I blew on the flame. I got a tiny smoulder going, then just smoke and soot. I was late for school. I'd need more time and more matches. I folded the singed pads up, put them in my pocket, and took them back up to my bedroom. I'd have to deal with them when I got home later.

Later, after school, I had not two, but four used sanitary pads to incinerate. Then there were, five, six, seven. I could not light them on fire. I checked the instructions again. *Incinerate after use,* the package insisted. All I can remember about becoming a woman is standing at the garden burner before and after school, crying with frustration.

Why didn't I ask Mum what to do with the pads? Why didn't she tell me what to do with them? She must have seen me out there by the burner. She must have known. But neither of us asked or said anything.

She did tell me about menstruation when I was nine. But Pete Morgan* started it. It was a lucky day, getting to sit beside Pete Morgan on the bus. His eyes were deep brown pools. I had a big crush on him.

"Do you know what your period is?" he whispered, leaning so close I could feel the words on my ear and neck.

"No. What?"

"You have to ask your mother. Tell her my sisters have got it."

Pete Morgan's sisters were my babysitters.

"Mum, what's a period? The Morgan girls have got one."

"Who told you that?"

"Pete Morgan. He said to ask you what it was."

**not his real name.*

Mum explained that when a girl grew up and became a woman she got a bit of blood in her underwear every month. This meant that when she got married she'd be able to have babies. Not before she was married. Only after she was married. The Morgan girls were starting to grow up. The blood was called a period. But they wouldn't have babies until they were married.

"It won't happen to you for years and years, so you don't need to worry about it. And don't talk to Pete Morgan or any boys about that again."

"Do you get the period, Mum?"

"Yes. And look, I've got four girls and another baby coming!"

I felt a bit squeamish about Pete Morgan after that. But my fascination with the Morgan girls skyrocketed. The next time Beth Morgan came to babysit, I sneaked up the hallway when she went to the toilet and listened outside the door, hoping to find out something about her period. All I heard was the sound of peeing.

After my first period finished, a couple of days after it started, I had a bag of used pads in a plastic bag under my bed, and they were starting to smell a tiny bit fishy.

I was saved by an institutional incinerator. It was in one of the bathrooms at school. I'd seen it before, but never made the connection between it and sanitary pads, until I was in desperate need of incineration. I read the instructions on the incinerator. *Insert sanitary pads one at a time, do not overload. Press the red button to incinerate. Empty ashes as needed.*

I got rid of all those pads in one go. Burnt to ashes, precisely as instructed.

At school we had a human biology lesson about puberty. I was aware of changes happening in my body. I found out that some adolescents experienced hormonal havoc, mood swings, boundary pushing and independence seeking, growing pains, sexual interest and exploration. But I didn't have any of that. I wasn't allowed to be like that.

"We can't stop you getting your period," was the silent message from Mum, "but it doesn't mean anything. We won't have any trouble from you. You're staying exactly the way you are."

And so adolescence became an extension of childhood. I did what I was told, kept my thoughts to myself, behaved myself. Once, in an attempt to appear to be a "normal" adolescent, I decided to become depressed. I began to mope and hang my head, took my grooming down a notch.

"What on earth's the matter with you?" Mum snapped on the second day.

"I'm depressed." I said, with feeling.

"What have *you* got to be depressed about?" she barked. "Go and hang out the washing if you need something to be depressed about!"

So I hung out the washing, and cheered up, to avoid any more unnecessary housework.

I look over at her. She's just sharp bones now, under a sheet. She has no breasts left, no flesh or fat anywhere on her now. She's disappearing in front of our eyes.

I get up and go over to the bedside. Ask her if she wants water. She nods. I help her lift her head up so she can sip from the baby cup.

Chapter 8
SEARCHING

"What are you reading, Susie?"

"Just an old journal I found up in the attic."

"Have you been writing about this?" My sister glanced over at Mum.

"No. I probably should. But I can't."

"It's hard eh?"

"Yeah. It is."

"What's in the journal?"

"Endless agony about boys. When I was 16."

She's lonely, the writer of that journal. She knows loads of people, but she's not close to anybody. She's got nobody to talk to—really talk to—except herself. She writes, "Hello, how's things?" to herself. "Sorry I didn't write yesterday." She knows it's a bit pathetic, writing to herself. But she needs to put her feelings somewhere. She longs for someone to understand her feelings. But there's nobody.

At 15 I joined Search, the local Catholic youth group. It was the only acceptable alternative to the other social activities on offer in my home town—driving around in cars, going to discos or parties, drinking, drugs, and having sex. The Search group didn't do any of that, at least not officially, so my parents let me go.

"Have you *found* anything yet?" Mum would ask when I got home from the Thursday night Search meeting. I'd roll my eyes. But I did find something at Search.

At Search I discovered a different God. Not the old man Catholic God with the long white hair and beard; not Jesus hanging on the cross with blood pouring out the wound near his heart and his head dripping from thorn stabbings. At Search I discovered Jesus Christ Superstar. Long brown hair, faded t-shirt and jeans, goatee, bare feet. I felt completely normal at Search. For the first time in my life.

We met at the Search House, a derelict wooden building beside the presbytery with sticky carpet, peeling wallpaper, rattling windows and doors. We slumped in cast-off couches and armchairs donated by parishioners, we discussed the meaning of life, we played our guitars and sang. There'd be a dozen or 20 of us at that house every Thursday night with the youth pastor, who was the parish priest wearing jeans and a t-shirt, goofing off with us instead of drinking and playing cards with our parents.

Search stretched my experience of Catholicism. At Search it was acceptable to question Catholic doctrine, to debate. I loved debating matters of faith—

especially because so much Catholic doctrine was irrational. I loved to point out the blatant problems of child baptism, limbo and purgatory, contraception bans, male-only entry to the priesthood, the institutionalized chauvinism.

At school, the Search girls stirred things up in Religious Education class. We knew the Bible, and it didn't always corroborate what the nuns taught us. The young nuns loved a good theological debate, but the older nuns wouldn't tolerate our heresies. "Faith, girls! You must have Faith when you have doubt. Pray to God for Faith!"

A Bishop visited our Religious Education class and I caused a stir by questioning infant baptism. How could a baby make an important choice like that, and what right did the parents and the Church have to make it for them? How could God, who is Love, banish an unbaptised baby to hell or limbo? Limbo's not even in the Bible. Word got back to my parents that I was mouthy and bold to the Bishop.

Mum was annoyed. "You can't go around questioning the Catholic faith, Susan! Not in front of a Bishop! It's the one true Church. You just *have* to believe it. That's what faith *is*. And you need to respect the clergy, whether you agree with them or not."

Dad just gave me a look that said there's no point arguing about this.

My parents opened our house up to all my Search friends. We had rooms large enough for 20 kids and their record player and guitars. I was expected to stay on top of my schoolwork. Otherwise I could socialize as much as I liked. As long as it was at home.

Nobody else's parents wanted gangs of teenagers hanging around. Mine seemed to love it. I realize now it was how they let me have a busy social life without letting me out of their sight.

Search was also a place I met lots of boys. I'm embarrassed and even a bit shocked at the number, frequency and intensity of my crushes on boys during this time. The journal drips with boy angst. I start writing the journal two weeks after my first kiss. It happened at Oreti Beach, in the back of a car. The kiss memory is scrambled. In the feeling memory I'm being crushed into the floor in the back of the car. It's cold and dark and sandy. But I know I wouldn't have been on the floor. It would have been the back seat. His mouth felt wet and open. It didn't feel at all lovely or warm or happy like I'd expected a kiss to be. It felt slimy. And yet… and yet I'd been kissed, finally. It must be love. I waited for that boy to phone, or visit or write. He didn't. Turned out he already had a girlfriend.

Another boy lent me his Scout jacket. Of course, I fell for him. Another taught me a song on the guitar. I fell for him next. I fell hopelessly in love with any boy who showed the slightest interest in me—six monumental crushes in the three months either side of my 16th birthday. I'd obsess about one boy until the next one flattered me with some small attention. I was totally passive. I would never have telephoned or approached any of these boys. I waited for a call, a visit, a sign I was special. I'd wait for days or weeks, agonizing about what they thought, what they meant by their silence.

The last boy I fell in love with during this time, loved me back. It was a huge relief—finally someone to really talk to, someone who "got" me, who understood.

We lived 40 miles apart. We wrote letters most days. That's probably why the journal ended when it did. I'd write to him instead of writing to myself. Dad mailed my outgoing letters from his office. Mum hid the incoming letters around the house. I'd come home from school and ask, "Any mail for me today?"

"Yes!"

"Where is it?"

"You'll have to find it."

It might be up by the ceiling, slid into the strings of the macramé pot plant hanger. I'd climb up on a bar stool, onto the kitchen counter, get it down. It might be sitting in the toaster. Did she once hide a letter under the fish bowl? I have a watery memory of my name and address smearing in the wake of a goldfish's tail. Why did she do these things? Did she want to make fun of it? She maybe just wanted to be part of it.

"Read it out loud to us! We all want to know what it says!"

"No!" I'd take my letter upstairs to read in my room. I'd reply immediately.

Mum and Dad embraced this boy. He was from a good Catholic family, went to Catholic school, played in the First Fifteen rugby team, so he was OK. They invited him to come and stay on weekends, to come on family outings and holidays. They seemed to like him a lot. *More than they liked me.*

He was outgoing. More sociable than I was. He was also opinionated. He and Mum enjoyed debating and winding each other up. *Like adults.*

I anguished about how embarrassing Mum was in front of my friends. She'd rush to answer the doorbell and put on some kind of clown act before letting them in. She'd challenge them to games and competitions. She'd lure them close to the kids' swimming pool then push them in. She'd tease them more, and they'd push her in.

I hated these antics.

"Why do you have to be so serious all the time, Susan? Stop scowling."

She'd pop into the living room when I had friends around, maybe wearing an ape mask or a wig, "Just making sure you're all behaving yourselves." My friends thought she was great, having boring grown-up parents of their own. Not me. I was mortified.

I remember getting up the courage to ask her, politely, if she would mind not being such a clown in front of my friends.

"If they didn't like it they wouldn't keep coming back." This rare lapse into brevity and logic surprised me. My friends did love coming to our place. It was so much more fun than anyone else's place. Everyone wanted parents like mine. *Everyone except me.*

I remember a warm Sunday afternoon, the Search group gathered at our place, my boyfriend and I sitting outside by the tree stump; he's playing the guitar, I'm singing. There are friends on the veranda. More friends inside in the lounge. I heard screams then raucous laughter from inside. I ran through the veranda doors, anxious to hush the commotion before it attracted Mum's attention.

I needn't have bothered. Mum was sitting at the piano playing Norwegian Lullaby, double speed in the wrong key. My little sister Angie, only six years old, was hypnotizing a chicken. She'd catch a chicken, bring it inside, hold its head in one hand like the vet showed her, and circle a finger around its beak while staring into its startled eyes. Within seconds it would pass out with its wings flopped by its side, ready for the vet's examination.

This day she didn't get a chance to wake the chicken up according to the vet's instructions. Maybe it was Mum's manic piano recital that broke the spell. The chicken snapped awake with a squawk, startled everyone with its frantic wing flapping. It dumped a large nervous poop on the carpet.

"Angie, take that chicken outside." Even though my friends were delighted with the performance, I wanted it over.

"Mum said I could bring it in."

"Well take it outside now. Mum. Stop that noise."

Everyone was laughing except me. *Party pooper. Killjoy. Stick-in-the-mud.*

I'm not sure this memory is 100 percent true. I don't honestly know if Mum was banging on the piano at the exact same time as Angie was hypnotising the chicken. Or even if it was on the same day. But these things did happen. More than once. And in front of my friends. Maybe they weren't clustered together in the mayhem I remember that day. But maybe they were.

Around this time I got an after-school job, had my own money, and discovered Salvation Army stores.

I started wearing men's tweed jackets, plain white cotton shirts and satin neck ties, long cotton skirts made from Indian block prints. And hats. All shapes and styles. Polyester and acrylic fibres had arrived in New Zealand, and the second-hand shops were flooded with excellent quality lambswool and cashmere sweaters and coats, silk suits, hand wash or dry clean only. I snapped them up, loving the exquisite fabrics, the fine tailoring. I'm sure I looked frightfully bohemian, and it must have grieved Mum mightily to watch me come downstairs in my latest outfit.

She would sigh, "You're not wearing *that* out are you?"

"Well, yes, I was thinking of wearing it." Internally rolling my eyes.

"Why can't you wear something pretty and flattering instead of those awful old things?"

"Because I don't want to tempt boys."

And she'd look offended. And I'd go out wondering if I looked as utterly cool as I felt, or totally ridiculous. I never quite knew.

My school friends, Search friends, my boyfriend, were applying for teaching or nursing college or university—all of which were out of town. They'd be leaving home. School was finishing in just a few weeks.

What was I going to do?

"What's wrong with staying here and getting a job?"

"Nothing's wrong with it, Mum. I just want more from my life."

"More what? What's wrong with staying here with your family?"

"I don't know. I want a career. I want to be a journalist."

"Then why don't you apply to the Southland Times. They take cadets don't they?"

I didn't want to be a cadet at the Southland Times. And work two doors down from my father's office. I wanted to study Journalism at Wellington Polytech. My English grades were excellent. I loved writing essays.

What I really wanted was to get away from home. But I couldn't say that.

At the dinner table, I'd manage to steer the conversation around to "what Susan's going to do when she leaves school".

"I really want to be a writer."

"You can't be a writer, just like that!"

"I'm a good writer."

"Why can't you just get a job in a good office? You're only 17."

"I'm thinking about applying for Wellington Polytech. The journalism programme."

Mum would put down her knife and fork, or her wine glass, whichever she was holding, drop her head, and start crying.

"You'll break up the family if you leave home."

"I'm only thinking about it."

Dad warned me when I first went to high school, to steer well clear of commercial subjects.

"Never take typing or shorthand, Susie. You'll just end up being Someone's Secretary."

He made it sound like the worst thing ever, and I quietly vowed I would never end up being Someone's Secretary. But it was Mum's ambition for me. A nice job in an Invercargill office. Living at home with the family. Dating a nice Invercargill boy, getting married and having kids. Preferably girls. Just like she did.

"But I really want to have a career. Girls can have careers now."

"What's wrong with having a family?"

"Nothing's wrong with it, Mum. It's just not what I want."

"Don't think a career's going to make you happy. You'll be lonely if you leave home. You won't know what's struck you."

The application forms arrived in the mail and I filled them out, first in pencil, then over the top in pen. Dad posted them from his office.

A few weeks later, there was a letter from Wellington Polytech waiting for me when I got home from school. Mum didn't hide it. She acted like she wasn't interested.

"I have to go for an interview."

"Go where? To Wellington? How are you going to get to Wellington for an interview?"

Excellent question. I had hardly any money of my own. I'd have to fly. I'd have to go alone to a strange city and find the Polytech. And find the right room.

My memory blanks at this point. Somehow I did fly to Wellington. I clearly remember getting off an airport bus on Lambton Quay. As my eyes adjust-

ed to the bright sunshine, I remembered my yellow backpack in the luggage hold under the bus, which had already pulled away from the stop and was half-way down the block.

"My backpack!" I yelled; my arms shot up in the air.

A man in a black suit spun around in his tracks, let out an impressive whistle, and sprinted after the bus. He caught up with it at the next set of traffic lights. I sprinted behind him. The driver opened the door, got out, and gave me my pack. I turned to thank the man in the suit, but he was gone.

Mum and Dad must have bought me that airfare. Dad would have talked Mum around. He would have said, "Susie will be fine. She's sensible. She can stay with the Morgans. They'll look after her."

I was fine. I found my way to the Reserve Bank and met my uncle, who took me home on the commuter train that night and brought me back to town for the interview the next morning. I found my way through Wellington to the Polytech. It was a day of tests and presentations with a large group of applicants for the Journalism programme. I loved it. Every bit of it, except the last session, when we were all tired, kicking back now it was almost over. A man in a suit came into the room. "Tell me about your media contacts," he smiled, pointing to a would-be journalist in the front row.

By the time it was my turn, I was almost too humiliated to speak. I had zero media contacts, and I was in a room full of people whose fathers ran news rooms for TV stations, who worked part time at their local radio station, or interned at their local papers. Many of them had plenty of media contacts. I knew nobody. Then I remembered. "I'm the editor of my school magazine."

"Alright, who's next?"

"How did it go, Susie?" Dad met me at the airport. "I nearly lost my pack on the bus in Wellington. But a man ran after the bus and stopped it. Don't tell Mum."

"That was lucky. How was the interview?"

"I'm sure I did well on the tests. But they wanted to know what media contacts we had, and I haven't got any."

"Don't worry, as long as you did your best."

When the envelope with the Wellington Polytech logo arrived, Mum left it on the counter in plain sight. I sprinted upstairs to my room to open it. This letter was going to change my life.

We regret to inform you... What? ... *that we cannot offer you a place in the 1979 Journalism programme at Wellington Polytech...* Hang on, that can't be right. English is my best subject. I got 100 percent for grammar. I always got an A for my essays.

And I did my best. A journalist, a real writer, was the only thing I wanted to be. That was my career. This was the only programme I'd applied for. No plan B. I'd never needed a plan B before.

Plan A was already playing out in my mind. I was already studying at the desk by the window in my Wellington hostel room. I was already going to Polytech every day, wearing whatever I wanted. I was meeting new people, doing new things. In my mind I had already left home.

Mum was clearly relieved when I came back downstairs crying, and put the rejection letter on the counter.

"Well at least you won't have to worry about moving to Wellington now. You can stay home and get a good job. There are lots of ads in the paper."

There were lots of ads in the paper. For secretaries. With no typing or shorthand skills, I was under no pressure to apply for them. Besides I didn't want to disappoint Dad.

Towards the end of the summer, when most of my friends and my boyfriend had moved away to start their studies, I slumped over the newspaper at the kitchen table, with a pen in my hand, reading then striking through the help wanted ads.

Laboratory Assistant. School leaver position. Training provided. That might work. It was at the freezing works in Makarewa, a few miles out of town.

Maybe I could rent an old farmhouse and live in the country. I could get chickens and have a vege garden.

Chapter 9
WORKING GIRL

If one more person comes into this bedroom and tells me what a perfect childhood we had I'm going to throttle them. And they need to shut up about how proud my parents are of me, too. It's bullshit. *Total bullshit.*

Maybe they were proud of me when I was a kid. I towed the line then, made myself useful. I tried very hard to be a good girl, and I was generally successful. But the cracks started to show when I left school and started work.

I got the Laboratory Assistant job. Mum was thrilled that I had a job so close to home; no need for me to leave and break up the family. Her dream was still intact. Dad was happy I wasn't going to be a secretary, and I would earn more than minimum wage. I didn't know what to expect. And nothing could have prepared me for the shock of my new job.

You could smell the freezing works before you could see it. If the wind was right, you could smell it from

North Road in Invercargill. A smell of animal and rot and burning. A hot stink. When we were little, we'd squeal for Dad to wind up the car windows when we passed by Makarewa. It smelled so bad.

It still stank when I started working there. But everyone who worked there got used to it, couldn't smell it after a while.

Freezing works. Slaughterhouse. Huge, dirty white factory for killing farm animals and turning them into roasts and chops, tallow, blood and bone-meal. Acres of white ceramic tiles, shining stainless steel equipment, awash in blood.

Here's what a freezing worker looked like first thing in the morning. Pure white overalls over a clean white t-shirt. White knee-high gumboots. White hard-hat. Around his waist (they were always men) was a leather belt hung with a stainless steel carving knife or two and a sharpening steel. He hadn't shaved. He swaggered into the works, up to his place on the chain. He stood all day in the steam and heat, cutting up animals, sheep or cows, until the siren blasted a call for morning smoko, lunch, afternoon smoko, and knock-off by which time he was covered in blood and bits of guts and meat.

After his shift, he stripped off his bloodied work clothes, stood under a hot shower, pulled on his jeans, sweatshirt and gumboots, and swaggered out to his big boat of a car, pulled out of the parking lot with his elbow out the window, blowing a cloud of cigarette smoke as he ripped up some gravel on the way out the driveway.

They made good money working at the freezing works. The meat workers union was well organised and known for being tough. Everything about the freezing works was tough.

On my first day at work, I got to see the chain—literally a mechanical chain that clinked along with dead animals hanging off it, passing dozens of men with knives and saws who cut throats, skinned, hacked off hooves and heads, opened bellies to disgorge the guts and organs, trimmed and cut until each carcass was clean and ready to hang in the freezing chamber.

My lab coat and gumboots were several sizes too big. My blue hard hat kept slipping down my forehead. My colleague was giving me the introductory tour. She'd already shown me around the lab, which was clean, orderly, cool, quiet. She warned me as we were putting on our boots and hats to go into the bowels of the freezing works, "They'll try to shock you and get a rise out of you. Just smile and keep walking. If they whistle or cat-call, just be friendly. It always happens when women go in there."

We walked across the courtyard flanked by the lab, the office, and the butcher shop. When she opened the door to the chain, a hot, steamy stink hit me in the face, wrapped itself around me like a heavy blanket. My eyes adjusted to the glaring fluorescent lights, the white, the steel, the blood. Blood ran through troughs in the floor; it splattered over everything.

The only sounds were the hiss of steam, the gentle clatter of the chain, the clink of knives on steel. Then a sharp shout, and a steady beat, the backs of knives on stainless steel, just a few, then a few hundred, drumming *women in the building*. They whistled and cat-called and banged their knives as my colleague pointed out the sterilizing baths we would test every day, the places to collect blood samples, the nurse's station. We were stared at and cheered and drummed through the vast room. A grizzly old hulk of a man walked towards us, holding up his knife dripping with blood, and licked slowly along its 8-inch blade as he winked right at me.

"God, that's gross," I winced.

"Keep smiling, keep walking. It's just a show. You have to have a sense of humour about it."

I managed a weak grin.

She waved at someone she knew and the whole place erupted in shouts and whistles.

We reached the far end of the room and pushed another heavy door into a cool windowless corridor, connected to other corridors, marked with signs: Laundry. First Aid. Fitter-Turners. Electricians. Meat Inspection. Production Manager. We slipped into the Production Manager's office and I slumped into a chair.

"That your first time on the chain?"

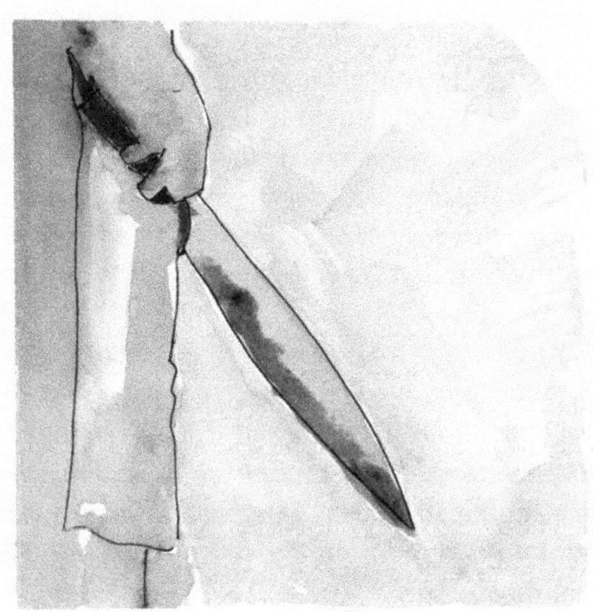

"Yeah."

"You'll be great. They love having a bit of fun in there. Don't take it seriously."

"OK."

Back in the lab I was overwhelmed with my new job. Chemistry. I was good with words, not numbers and formulas. And all the new people. Dozens of men, all in white with varying degrees of blood splattering, popped in all day to "meet the new girl".

I had no idea there were so many men in the world. They were all so friendly. And I was terrified of them.

"How was your first day at work, Susie?" Dad was proud of having a daughter in the workforce.

"Pretty good. I got to walk down the chain."

"Hope they behaved themselves." Dad had worked at the freezing works when he was younger. Pretty much every male I knew had worked there when they needed a well-paid job and didn't care what it was.

"They made a bit of noise. But it was OK."

"What sort of work are you going to be doing?"

"I have to collect samples from different places around the works, and do tests on them to make sure they meet the standards. Like bonemeal. And dried blood. I write a report and give it to the boss. That's all really."

"They're a good employer. It's a good place to get your first job. When's pay day?"

"It's only once a month, on the third Thursday. I'll get a cheque."

"You'll need to get a proper bank account now. I'll take you to the bank one day if you can come into town at lunch time."

"Thanks Dad. Will I get my own cheque book?"

"Sure will. Good thing I taught you how to balance one!"

"Yep. You sure did."

"Susan's a freezing worker," Mum laughed, "She says she's in the laboratory, but she's really working on the chain."

Men. Males. Hundreds, maybe a thousand of them. It was a man's world at the freezing works. There were a couple of women working in the office, a couple of us in the lab, and Nursie. That's what they called Florence McCoy, the nurse who cleaned and dressed their inevitable cuts. The office girls, the lab girls, and Nursie.

We were magnets for the men. They popped in all day for a chat, a smoke, a sit down in our little staff room. We talked and laughed. I got comfortable among them. Some were protective, like a brother might have been I supposed. Some were flirty. Some were shy. Some were predatory. I was whistled at and cat-called most days. I was grabbed a few times, kissed against my will once. When that happened I was so shocked. I wondered what I'd done to cause it—I always dressed modestly, tried not to be too friendly. I realised it was impossible not to tempt boys in a place like that. Just being there was asking for trouble.

All my close friends had left town. My boyfriend moved to Wellington. We broke up. I stopped going to Search. No point with my friends all gone. I started hanging out with people I met at work.

A boy from the Trades department asked me out. He picked me up on Friday nights and drove me back to Makarewa, to the Green Roofs pub, where I flashed my fake ID, ordered a shandy—half larger, half lemonade, the only acceptable lady's drink in a scungy country bar—and learned how to play pool. When the bar closed we'd pile into his car and speed down the road to a house party. Afterwards he'd drop me home. I was 19. I don't remember having a curfew any more, but I was expected to come home and alone.

Mum didn't like this boy. She complained he wasn't sociable. He didn't make good eye contact. He didn't come to the house to hang out with the family. He didn't kid around with her. He didn't like her either. Looking back, I can see her judgment was sound; but at the time, their mutual dislike and distrust was fine with me.

One night, as I was getting out of the car, he reached over and pulled the passenger door closed.

"You know, I've been taking you out for three months now. It's time we started having sex."

I'd hoped to stay a virgin until I met someone I wanted to marry. I didn't expect to wait until I had a wedding ring on, but I wanted to have the intention of marrying the man I first had sex with. And I did not want to marry this one. I did not want to live in Makarewa, married to a tradesman who drank at the Green Roofs most nights. I did not want to end up with a bunch of rugby-playing kids, and be a housewife. My social life might have hit rock bottom in a few short months, but I had no intention of staying down here. I was going to be a writer. One day. One day I was going to get out of here.

But I didn't say that.

"OK. Just give me a few weeks. I don't want to get pregnant."

"OK, but not too long."

I talked to my colleague, only a couple of years older than me, but much more worldly and experienced with men. She gave me a book about sex. Not a Catholic book warning about sex. A non-Catholic book full of information about how to have sex, what to expect, both good and bad. It was riveting. She also told me about the Family Planning Clinic.

"I can't go there, can I?" I knew people who picketed the Family Planning Clinic.

"Anyone can go there! You just ring up and make an appointment."

She talked to me, woman to woman, about sex. It's just as well. I had no idea what I was in for. I had never even seen an adult penis. I was becoming far more nervous than excited. I was really only doing this because it felt like it was about time. I was 19. Virginity gets to be a burden by that age.

And I did hope, secretly, that if we had sex the relationship might improve, get a bit more personal, you know, closer.

I rang the clinic and made an appointment. Just like that. There was no inquisition, just a date and a time. When I arrived it was just like a regular doctor's office, except all the posters were about contraception, sex and STDs. There was a baby screaming in the waiting room. When the mother was called in for her appointment, I said "I'll take him for you.

Don't worry, I'm good with babies." She handed him over and I got him comfortable and quiet. You need to hold them tight enough so they feel safe, but not too restricted. They need their head and neck supported. They like the rhythm of walking slowly. Mum taught me so much about looking after babies.

"You've done that before, haven't you?" the receptionist smiled.

"I had four little sisters to look after."

The doctor called me in for my appointment.

"What can we do for you today, Susan."

"Well, umm, I want to have sex with my boyfriend, and I don't want to get pregnant. I thought I should go on the pill."

"That's sensible. Are you having sex already? Could you be pregnant?"

"No. I'm still a virgin."

"OK. Will it be hard for you to remember to take a pill every day? There are other options we can talk about."

"No, I'll remember. I've read up about it and I think the pill would be best for me."

"Alright. I'll write you a script. You can get it filled at any pharmacy. You get repeats whenever you need them. There's no cost. Is there anything else you need?"

"Umm, no. Is that it?"

"Yes. Here's your script. Good for you for thinking about contraception in advance."

Holy Shit! I walked out, just like that, with a prescription for the pill. I couldn't believe it. They didn't lecture me, make me explain myself, try and talk me out of it, or flatly refuse me. I was gob-smacked. I think this might have been the first time in my life I'd asked for something and just got it. It was certainly the first time in my life I felt taken seriously about an important decision. They treated me like an adult. They *praised* me for wanting to go on the pill.

I read and re-read the fine print on the pill packaging, took a tiny blue pill every morning when I woke up, and waited for the recommended two weeks for the hormones to start working.

When I was sure I was safe, I told my boyfriend I would be ready on Friday after work. I got dressed up specially in my favourite magenta overalls and white t-shirt, red strappy sandals. He took me back to his place after work, showed me my first adult penis, showed me what to do with it, and a couple of hours later I was home eating dinner with the family. Glowing, I imagined. But burning down there like you wouldn't believe. It had hurt like hell.

After dinner, I rang him up to talk about this miraculous development in our relationship.

"He's gone to the pub for the night. Said he'd be back tomorrow."

"Really? Umm. OK."

I needed someone to talk to. I rang my friend from work.

"Did you do it?"

"Yup!"

"Was it OK?"

"Yup. But it really hurt."

"Well it does the first time. You'll be fine now."

"He's gone to the pub tonight."

"Doesn't he always go out to the pub on Friday night?"

"Yes, but I thought he wouldn't go tonight."

"Why not?"

"I don't know. I just thought he'd stay home, you know, because of what happened."

"Don't be silly! He's a guy. He'll be bragging to his friends by now!"

She didn't mean to be hurtful, and I knew I was being naive. But still.

I went to bed early. That first sex was easily as disappointing as my first kiss. How could it have been otherwise? All I wanted was to be close and special to some other human, for the loneliness to go away. All I felt was desolate, bleak.

It didn't take Mum long to figure out what was going on.

One morning I saw her on the upstairs landing, eyes red and puffy, jaw jutting out like only hers could, angry, helpless, beside herself.

"What's the matter?" I asked, genuinely concerned.

She wouldn't speak; she rushed into her room and shut the door.

I went downstairs to the kitchen.

"Dad, what's wrong with Mum?"

"Perhaps you should go up and talk to her. She's pretty upset with you."

"With me? Why? I haven't done anything."

"Just go and talk to her."

I took my coffee and went upstairs, fearing nothing, suspecting nothing but a minor misunderstanding.

"What's the matter, Mum?"

She reached over to her bedside table, picked up a small package, and held it out.

"What. Are. These?" she shook with rage.

She was holding my contraceptive pills.

"Umm. It's the pill. Where did you get them from?"

"Your toilet bag. What are you doing with these? I knew there was something wrong with you lately. You've been moody and distant! What are you doing with these? Where did you get them?"

"I'm taking them to regulate my periods. For PMS."

"YOU don't have PMS!" she roared. "Where did you get them!? Not from Doctor Pottinger?"

Doctor Pottinger was the Good Catholic doctor in town. No contraceptive pills available there.

"I went to a different doctor."

"You are NOT going to be on the pill. It's a mortal sin. I'm throwing these away! If you've got problems with your period, we can go to Doctor Pottinger. Is that clear?"

"Alright."

I left the room and went to check on my toilet bag. It was hidden well away in the bottom drawer of my dresser. The pills were gone.

When I got to work I phoned the Family Planning Clinic to get another prescription. I'd hide them better this time.

One of the perks of being on staff at the freezing works was a free shuttle service from home to Makarewa every day. The other perk was having plenty of my own money. The first thing I bought was my own sewing machine, so I didn't have to ask to borrow Mum's. Then I bought my own car, so I didn't have to ask to borrow Mum's. The taste of freedom was heady.

"I'm going to start looking for my own place soon," I announced over dinner one night.

"What do you mean, your own place?"

"I thought I'd rent a farm house in Makarewa. I could have a big vege garden and chickens."

"For goodness sake, Susan, what's wrong with living here with your family? You can have a vege garden here if you want one."

"Nothing's wrong with it. I just want my own place. I'm 19 now. You were getting married and getting your own place when you were 19."

"Well I was getting married. That's completely different from living on your own. A girl shouldn't live alone. Especially not in a house in Makarewa. It's rough out there."

"I'm just thinking about looking."

"I don't understand why you're so keen to leave the family. You don't know how lucky you've got it."

I stayed living at home. When I turned 21, Mum and Dad threw a big 21st birthday party for me. The song says, "You've got the key to the door, never been 21 before." I got a key. But it didn't make any difference.

I was desperate to leave. I felt I couldn't leave just because I wanted to be free. I needed a good reason. I got it one weekend when I went skiing and met a group of students my own age who were all in the third year of their Bachelor of Arts degrees. They spent their days reading books and writing essays. They were interesting. Intelligent. Funny. They were happy. They were who I wanted to be.

"I've enrolled in the English department at Canterbury University."

"You've what?"

"I'm going to university to study English. I've got enough money saved to pay the fees, and I can get a bursary for my living expenses."

"What's wrong with your job? You're making great money and you have good benefits." Even Dad disapproved. "You'll end up with a degree and a poor paying job in a government department. I bet you'll earn less with an English degree than you do now at the freezing works." He was absolutely right. But still, I had more immediate problems to solve. Like getting away from home.

"I've already been accepted. I'm going to Christchurch at the end of January."

"But where are you going to live?"

"I'll get a flat."

"Can't you do it closer? Don't they have English at Otago University?"

"They do, but I want to go to Christchurch. They have a better programme there."

That wasn't true. I wanted to go to Christchurch because it was further away. It wouldn't be feasible to come home for weekends. It was a safe distance.

Three months later, I was nestled into an old armchair in my flat. I'd bought a book on vegetarian cooking, and had made a chunky grain salad that I scooped out of a funky pottery bowl I found at a Salvation Army shop. I was reading one of the books from the pile that towered beside my bed. I could hardly believe my luck. My "job" for the next three years was to read literature, discuss it and write about it. I was taking some Classics courses too, and Political Science. Heaven.

It was about seven o'clock. The sun was setting. My flatmate was studying in his room. This was the me I was meant to be. I had space and time to be. To become. To be a reader and writer. To become a vegetarian. To be alone, and OK with alone. To feel normal. And I did. I felt relaxed and normal, like I'd never felt before.

The doorbell buzzed. My flatmate answered it.

"Sue, it's for you."

An old friend of my parents stood on the doorstep.

"Hi Susie, how are you?"

"I'm great, John. How are you?"

"I've just come up from Invercargill. I've got a parcel for you in the car. Come out and get it."

The setting sun glared on the car windows. There was someone in the passenger seat, but I couldn't see who it was until the door opened.

"Surprise!" Mum beamed, "I've come to visit!"

She couldn't have known how upset I was. I was expert at hiding my feelings.

She brought in her suitcase, settled into my room, slept in the double bed with me, and wanted to come to my classes with me the next day.

"That's all a bit too brainy for me," she announced in the cafeteria after a Renaissance Poetry lecture. My new friends all laughed. I squirmed in my plastic seat. I squirmed because I was embarrassed. But mostly I squirmed because in that moment I loathed my mother—and that was a complicated, deeply uncomfortable feeling.

That same feeling creeps up all the time as I sit at her bedside.

I realize we've done a fairly good con job over the years—keeping up appearances. We don't fight or battle. We're civil. We're exceedingly careful with each other. We wobble, almost imperceptibly, on a tightrope, trying, trying not to fall.

Chapter 10
CATHOLIC

It started to feel like Mum really was going. Not dead, yet, but not really there any more. Faded out, like the old photos. Only occasionally in sharp focus. Just last night, she surprised me with a flash of lucidity. *Acidity.*

All five of us sisters were in her room, sitting on the floor going through the photo box again. We were drinking wine. A party in Mum's room. Mum was a shadow under her navy blue sheet. She might have been listening or she might have been knocked out with morphine. We didn't know. But we knew she'd be happy to have us all there together. She loved having all her girls in one place. This might be the last time.

She stirred and tried to sit up. Maria decided we should each say goodbye to her, give her a chance to say something before she died. We went over one at a time. When it was my turn, I sat rigid on the side of the bed, not touching Mum and not looking at her. Maria pushed me over onto Mum's pillow, and somehow got Mum's arms around my neck. I had nothing to say, but Mum was ready for me.

"I used to think that you leaving the Catholic Church was the worst thing that ever happened in my life. But now I realise it doesn't matter." Her arms dropped away. I got up. Poured another glass of wine, an extra big one, slumped into the rocking chair. Furious.

The night Dad died, he called each of us into this room, alone, to say goodbye. He said to me, "You were always kind and loving, Susie, even when you were a little kid. And you still are." It was a shock to hear that from Dad; he'd never said anything soft and sensitive like that before. But it wasn't as shocking as hearing I was responsible for the worst thing that ever happened in my mother's life.

All I could think was, "Of course it doesn't matter. My faith or lack of it has *nothing* to do with you!"

I picked up a wedding photo. I'm the bride in the polyester dress. Mum's in pink. She looks tense, smiling but rigid. I look wide-eyed, naïve. The only part of us touching are the hems of our dresses. Who knew it was the worst day of her life.

She must have been talking about the wedding. That was when the whole Catholic thing blew up. I was in my final year at university. I was dating my old high school sweetheart again.

He and I left Christchurch early on Friday afternoon and drove the six hours to my parents' place, so he could ask them if he could marry me. We thought it would be a nice touch, doing it the old-fashioned way, even though we had already decided. Mum and Dad were relaxing with drinks by the fire when we arrived. It wasn't unusual that we'd show up at either of our families' places together. We'd stayed friends. But nobody knew we were dating again. That would be a surprise.

We chatted, caught up on the family news. Dad yawned and said, "I'm off to bed."

"Could you wait just a moment." Gerard stood up. "I've got something to ask you."

Dad sat down.

"I want to ask you if I could marry your daughter." There was a tiny silence.

"Which one?" Mum blurted. We all laughed, but I wished we hadn't indulged her.

"This one." He took my hand.

"Oh," Mum laughed, "Well you know we have plenty more daughters to choose from, if you'd like a different one!"

"Sue's the one for me."

Another tiny silence.

"What church will you get married in?" That was Mum again. Dad hadn't said anything yet.

"We haven't decided all the details yet, Rosie." How could he be so calm? "We've only just decided to get married this week. But we'll most likely have our pastor at Spreydon Baptist say the vows."

"You mean it won't be a Catholic wedding? Is that what you're saying?"

"No, not as such. We would be happy to have your priest join in if you like."

Dad piped in, "Well Gerard, you're like one of the family already, I'm sure… "

"But Peter! They're not having a Catholic wedding!" Mum started crying.

I felt myself dissolving. I vaporised out of my body, up to the ceiling where I could see but not feel what was going on. I saw Mum crying and bewildered about why we couldn't just be Catholics like we were born and raised. Gerard stayed calm and respectful, firm. Dad was reasonable. I don't know if I spoke or not.

Eventually Dad went to bed. Mum stayed up for another round. Then she went to bed too. Gerard and I sat by the fire, talking quietly. I was back in my body, feeling again. This wasn't going to be easy, but we were facing it together.

To this day, I don't know if my parents ever said yes.

A month out from the wedding they called in the parish priest.

I waited for him in the big living room. It felt odd to be alone in that room. It was the scene of our family's social life, a place for rowdy card games, parties, limbo and Twister. That day it was deathly quiet, just the fire spitting lazily. I sat in Dad's chair.

I want to say that Mum sat me there, put my knees and feet into a lady-like arrangement, swept my hair behind my ears, and looked me over and sighed, "Be polite to Father Ives, alright?" There would have been tears in her eyes. Her chin would have been hard, jutting, quivering. But that didn't happen. I just went in on my own, sat down and waited.

He came to the front door. I heard Mum rush from the kitchen, through the hallway, to let him in. I heard a mumble of conversation. The living room door opened and he slipped in alone. Smaller than I remembered him. Older. Shabbier.

"Hello Susan. Good to see you."

"Hi Father." He sat opposite me, in Mum's chair, shuffling it closer.

"How are you, Susan?"

"I'm OK thanks. And you?"

"Me? Well I'm fine of course."

The fire spat. I felt we should be getting on with a game of darts, or poker.

"What's this about getting married outside the Church, Susan? You know that's why I'm here?"

"We're getting married at the new Victoria Chambers, Father. It's upstairs at the Civic Theatre. It will be the first wedding held there."

"But it's not a house of God, Susan. It's not a church."

"I know that, Father. We don't want to get married in a church."

"Why not? You're both Catholics. Good Catholic families. Surely you'd have a Catholic wedding?"

"I'm not a practicing Catholic any more Father. Neither is Gerard."

"So your mother tells me. But you could still get married in the Church. I would officiate. I married your mother and father you know."

"Yes I know."

"So how about it? Once a Catholic always a Catholic, eh?"

"It would be hypocritical Father."

"Hypocritical? What do you mean?"

"I'm not going to stand up in front of my family and friends and say things I don't believe."

"Like what?"

"Mainly making a vow to have children and bring them up in the Catholic faith. I don't even know if I want children. And if I did have them, I wouldn't bring them up as Catholics."

"You realize if you don't get married in the Catholic Church, it won't be a valid marriage? We won't recognize it."

"No, I didn't know that. But it will be legal. We have a Baptist pastor who's a certified marriage celebrant."

"So your mother tells me. And this Baptist fellow is willing to marry you at the… the Chambers?"

"Victoria Chambers. Yes."

"Your parents are very unhappy about this you know. It would mean a great deal to them if you just got married in the parish church. It would be a lot easier on your whole family. I've had a number of your relatives come to me about this already."

"Really? Why?"

"To get permission to go to this wedding—if it's not in a Catholic Church."

"They need permission?"

"Yes, of course. If a Catholic gets married outside the Church, other Catholics can't attend without their priest's permission. It makes it awkward for all of us. It's not a valid marriage. You'll be living in sin you know. Everyone has that on their conscience."

"Oh. So that's what the fuss is about."

"So you'll reconsider?"

"Umm, no. I'm not going to go through a performance of a Catholic wedding for appearances."

"What about your own faith? You've had a good Catholic upbringing."

"Father, my faith has changed. I don't believe the Catholic Church is the one true faith. I believe every faith is valid. I'm not anti-Catholic. Neither is Gerard. And because we have so many Catholic relatives, we'd like you to join in our wedding, along with our pastor. At the Victoria Chambers."

"I can't officiate at a wedding in a public hall with a Baptist pastor. Good Lord."

"We thought it would be a good compromise."

"No, I can't have anything to do with it if it's not at the parish church. Catholics must marry in the Catholic Church, or it's not a valid marriage."

"Well, we're not Catholics, so it doesn't matter I suppose."

"Once a Catholic, always a Catholic, Susan. If you marry outside the Church you'll be in a state of sin. You won't be able to receive Communion."

"Will you excommunicate me?"

"It probably won't amount to that."

"Mum will be pleased about that at least."

"You won't change your mind?"

"No Father. I'm following my conscience on this one."

"Well, there's nothing more I can do with you. I'd better talk to your mother."

He heaved out of the chair, and sighed his way into the kitchen. Facing Mum with the bad news was going to be worse than facing me with my bad faith.

Mum wouldn't speak for the rest of the day. It was the first time in my 23 years that I had stood up to her. *But not to her face. Coward.*

"What did Mum say to you, Susie?"

"What did she say to you?"

"She said I could be a nasty little bitch when I felt like it!" Ange snorted a laugh. "What did she say to you?"

"That me leaving the Catholic Church was the worst thing that ever happened to her."

"Really? I never thought *you'd* be the one to do the worst thing. You were always such a good girl!"

I was good. At everything except being a Catholic.

My faith started to fall apart not long after I started school, when I discovered my guardian angel was a traitor. The school bus dropped me at the corner of Patterson Street and Harvey Street, just six houses from home. My school case heavy. I was only five, but I knew I couldn't go home with a full lunch box. I crossed the street to the paddock we called the Long Grass, opened my case, took out the lunch box, shook out the dry vegemite sandwiches, the bruised apple far too big for my small mouth, a lump of cheese. Put the lunch box back in the case and crossed the street, into the side gate, up the back stairs into the laundry. Mum opened the door into the kitchen. She was cool. Not happy to see me.

"How was your day at school?"

"Good."

"How was your lunch?"

"Good."

"Did you eat it all?"

"Umm. Yes."

"Was it good? Did you like the sandwiches I made you?"

"Yes."

"Are you telling the truth?"

"Umm."

"Come with me."

She marched me over the road and pointed into the long grass.

"Whose lunch is this?"

"Mine."

"You lied to me, Susan. First you sneaked behind my back, then you lied. You know better than to lie to your mother. Pick up that lunch."

I couldn't find the words to tell her a whole apple was too big for my mouth. Even now I gag on a whole apple. I slice them with a pocket knife, thin and juicy. I couldn't tell her the sandwiches she hated making were dry, too big, the butter lumped not spread.

Later my sisters and I would laugh about those "angry sandwiches". Mum's most hated chore, making the school lunches. She'd forget about the lunches. Every day. The bread would still be in the freezer. She'd chip the slices apart with a knife, breaking some. She'd crush fridge-cold butter onto the frosty slices. It lumped and broke. And then vegemite, sometimes a piece of iceberg lettuce, sometimes a slice of cheese. A frozen slice of bread on top. If she tired to cut them, they'd chip and crack, so she left them whole. Too big.

"It will be thawed by lunch time. You'll have the freshest sandwiches at school."

I wanted jam sandwiches cut into triangles. Or any filling. But definitely triangles. They looked so pretty in other kids' lunch boxes. Their mothers weren't angry.

"Your guardian angel knows when you sin, Susan. Remember that next time you sneak behind my back and tell lies."

My guardian angel told Mum what I did? This was shocking news. I thought God gave me this angel when I was born to look after me. Just me. I used to go to sleep with my guardian angel's wings wrapped around me, cosy and happy that she was just mine. And now she tells on me to Mum.

"You can wait till Dad gets home for your punishment."

Mum talked to Dad. Dad called me over. Not icy. Sat me on his knee and talked. He was serious, gentle, calm, reasonable. I couldn't bear it. The kindness in his firm voice, the huge knowing he was in charge; as long as he was here it will all be OK.

"It's not the lunch that disappoints me, Susie. It's that you lied to Mum about it."

I couldn't bear to hear him say I'd disappointed him.

"Dad? Couldn't you just smack me and let me go?"

Dad burst out laughing and jiggled me off his knee. "Have you learned your lesson?"

"Yes. I'd rather have a smack than be growled at by you!"

Dad told that story so many times. The day Susie asked for a smack.

Jesus shocked me almost as badly as my guardian angel. One Sunday at Mass he started swinging around a big golden bowl on a chain. Smoke was pouring out and I worried the whole place would burst into flames. Nobody else seemed to notice.

"Mum."

Mum swatted me. You're not allowed to talk in Mass.

"But Mum! What's Jesus doing?"

Mum bent down and whispered in my ear. "That's not Jesus. It's Father Gaffey. Now be quiet."

Father Gaffey? If I'd been a bit naughtier I might have exclaimed, "Jesus Christ Almighty!"

Jesus was Father Gaffey? Father Gaffey was Jesus? No way.

Every Sunday we were dressed up and herded off to Mass to "see Jesus and pray to Jesus and offer it up to Jesus". And every Mass there was a man of roughly Jesus appearance, wearing a long gown, surrounded by stained glass windows and statues and candles, raising his arms to heaven, proclaiming Our Father and all other manner of Jesus-y behaviours. Everyone in the church praying and kneeling and bowing and crossing themselves.

If that was just Father Gaffey, where in the world was Jesus?

One day, Jesus was in my desk at school. I had just turned five. It was nearly time for the Christmas holidays.

I thought it best to put the three wise men and the two angels at the back of my desk, tucked in a corner, facing into the middle. The donkeys, with a little bit of straw to eat, went in the other back corner. Mary and Joseph should be together in the front, diagonally opposite the wise men and angels, and the sheep should be opposite the donkeys. Baby Jesus obviously went right in the middle. He was lying on his back waving his arms and legs in the air like a happy baby. He was happy, I imagined, because my father had made him a special manger out of popsicle sticks. No one else had a manger quite so flash.

There was nothing else in my desk. Just the nativity scene. I put down the lid, folded my arms and put my head down to take a rest. I thought about Baby Jesus in the middle, happy and smiling, sleeping.

"Open your desk, Susan," Sister interrupted my daydream.

I proudly lifted the lid.

"Put out your hand!"

I did it without thinking. You always did what the nuns told you.

Swack! Swack!

Some kids sniggered. Tears spurted from my eyes, not from the sting of the leather strap on my small hand, but because I was in trouble with Sister for the first time, and I didn't know what I'd done wrong. Some of the boys got strapped every day, but we always knew why. They swore or threw stones or laughed during prayers. I was always good.

"I told you to tidy your desk! Tidy up this mess right away! I'll be back to check it shortly."

I didn't know what to do. I bent my head down behind the desk lid, and cried on Jesus. Should I put all the figures in a straight line? Or in a circle? I didn't know. The nativity scene we had at home was in the fireplace, and it was stuffed with straw and angels and donkeys and sheep, and it even had a Santa—with his boots and legs dangling down from inside the chimney. It had presents wrapped in gold and red paper, and it had lights all around it. We said our prayers there at night during December, and one night before Christmas we'd be allowed to sleep in front of it in our sleeping bags with the lights twinkling all night. And then our Santa presents would miraculously be there when we woke up on Christmas morning.

Sister was making her way back up the row, checking every desk. I grabbed Mary, Joseph, the wise men and the angels and stuffed them in one apron pocket. I put the straw, the donkeys and the sheep in the other pocket. And I picked up Jesus in his popsicle stick manger and cradled him in my stinging hand. I whispered to him I was taking him home; he didn't need to live in a desk anymore.

Sister had nothing to go on this time. The desk was empty, and my hands were busy protecting the Son of God under my desk. She nodded as she put the lid down, and moved on to the next desk.

At school the nuns tell us we must ask God if we have a Vocation. Boys could be priests or religious brothers. Girls could only be nuns. God wants at least one vocation for every family in the parish, and I think it goes without saying that the oldest child in the family should try to be the Vocation.

I wanted to be our family's vocation, just like Aunty Judy. We call her Aunty Sister. She's not a missionary nun. She's a Dominican nun. She lives in a convent with other nuns and they're all school teachers. Her dress is long and white, with a black veil. The only way we can see her is to go to the Convent on Sunday afternoon, and wait quietly in the visitors' room. She comes in with some other nuns and we kiss her lovely soft cheek. We have to kiss the other nuns too, which we'd rather not, but you can't say no to a nun.

Mum took us to the convent to see Aunty Sister the day after I committed my first deadly sin. Gluttony. She told all the nuns about that sin. I hadn't had a chance to go to Confession, so I was still guilty. And ashamed to death.

At least I finally had a real sin to tell at Confession. We went to Confession every week, and I hardly ever had a real sin to tell, so I had to make them up. I picked from the examples sins from the Catechism book. My favourite was, "I stole money from my mother's purse," which sounded like the most terrifying sin in the world. I wouldn't ever dare do that. But I confessed it and the priest believed me. "Three Hail Marys and three Our Fathers, and promise never to do it again."

"Yes Father."

Genuflect. Kneel in the pew and say the penance. Leave church sin-free.

Having the sin of gluttony to confess meant I didn't have to lie to Father. Lying to Father was definitely a sin. But it was unavoidable if you were good and didn't have a real sin to tell every week.

"Bless me Father for I have sinned. It has been one week since my last Confession. Since that time I have committed the sin of gluttony."

Father didn't say anything for a moment. "The sin of gluttony?"

"Yes Father."

"And how did you do that?"

"Mum said I could eat whatever I wanted for lunch, so I picked a can of condensed milk and I ate half the can and threw up and Mum said it was gluttony. She even told the nuns."

"I see. And do you promise not to do that again?"

"Yes Father. I hate condensed milk now."

"Three Hail Marys and three Our Fathers."

"Yes Father." Genuflect.

I had to lie to the nuns, too. And to a Cardinal. We had to pick our Patron Saint for Confirmation. We studied the saints and picked the one we most wanted to be like. I picked Saint Francis of Assisi because he always had a bird on his hand and a lamb or a baby deer curled up at his feet. He was really nice to animals.

"Tell the class who you've chosen as your Patron Saint and why. Susan Ward?"

"Saint Francis. Of Assisi. Because of the animals he loved."

"Susan, Saint Francis of Assisi is a man."

"Yes Sister."

"And you're a girl."

"Yes Sister."

"So what does that tell you?"

"Nothing Sister."

My classmates giggled.

"Susan Ward. A *girl* cannot have a *man* as her Patron Saint. Go back to the book and pick a woman saint. There are plenty to choose from."

I was only nine, but I knew this was wrong. I wanted Saint Francis of Assisi because of the animals. Who cares if he's a man or a woman? But you can't argue with the nuns.

Did Mum or Dad give me the idea? They must have; I'm sure I didn't think it up myself. I looked up the Pocket Book of Saints and found a female Saint Frances. Patron Saint of motorists. She was approved by Sister, and her name was inscribed on my Confirmation certificate. But in my heart I picked Saint Francis of Assisi. Even when I was kneeling in front of the Cardinal getting confirmed, I said in my heart my name was Susan Maree Francis of Assisi, because he was the one I really wanted. The nuns and the Cardinal could believe what they liked.

A few years later the nuns were allowed to leave the convent on Sunday afternoons and go visiting. They came in a car, usually with a man from the parish who volunteered to drive them around.

They drove up the driveway, opened the car windows, and we crowded around and kissed them through the windows. Then mum brought out a tray with cups of tea and passed them to the nuns in the car. When they went to visit at Nana Baird's place, there was no driveway, so the car parked at the curb on Kelvin Street and Nana brought the tea tray right out to the street. I did not want to be that kind of nun. Allowed out of the convent, but not allowed out of the car. What if they had to go to the toilet?

"Bless me Father for I have sinned. It's been one week since my last confession. I've been thinking about the nuns peeing."

Every night we'd say our prayers before we went to bed.

Gentle Jesus meek and mild
Look upon a little child
Make me holy as thou art
And with thy love inflame my fart!

Even thinking something naughty was a sin. "Bless me father…"

Aunty Pat taught us a way to make sure we went straight to heaven if we died in our sleep. You just needed to sleep with your arms crossed over your heart all night. That way if you died God would know you were a Catholic and take you straight to heaven. I always crossed my arms over my heart when I went to bed. And every morning when I woke up they'd be uncrossed. I wasn't much of a Catholic. At least I hadn't died and ended up in purgatory, or worse, hell. Which was where you landed if you even thought about sinning and died before you got to Confession.

The day after my fireside chat with Father Ives, Mum woke up transformed. The whole business of the

Catholic wedding was never mentioned again. She took the reins and made sure the first wedding in the newly-renovated Victoria Chambers in the Civic Theatre was a huge hit. She organised the food and flowers and table settings. She made her own dress, and probably dresses for my sisters, too. Everyone agreed it was a lovely wedding. Only a handful of people knew the wedding dress was scratchy polyester, with a pair of hated high heels hidden under its flounces. The flower basket was loaded with Mrs Phillips' mock orange which bloomed at exactly the right moment. There was plenty of food, plenty of relatives and friends. The Baptist pastor charmed the Catholic crowd.

We heard on the family grapevine that Nana Ward approved of the Queen and King of Hearts being married by a Baptist—as her Sid was raised Baptist. He'd had to convert to Catholicism to marry Nana, and lost his inheritance in the process. I got the feeling she thought this wedding was putting the record right between the extended family Baptists and the Catholics.

Dad was gobsmacked that there was so much booze left over after the wedding. He'd done the wine and beer catering himself, basing his calculations on the usual Ward family party consumption. He didn't know that most of our friends and the other side of the family were not big drinkers. Many didn't drink at all. So Dad got to take more than half the booze home afterwards, which perhaps more than made up for any trouble we'd caused.

We were heading out on a motorcycle trip for our honeymoon. I asked Mum why she'd been silent on the subject; I'd expected a loud protest. She looked me straight in the eye and said, "Now that you're married, you're Gerard's responsibility, not mine."

Mum's funeral would be a Requiem Mass at St Theresa's parish church. There would be a whole herd of priests on the altar—they'd come from all over the country. Even Father Ives would be there. There would be standing room only in the huge church.

Chapter 11
BITTEN

"David's coming, Mum. He's arriving tomorrow."

I didn't expect her to answer. She'd been drifting in and out of consciousness. But she perked right up, opened her eyes wide in mock shock.

"Do you think he still loves you?"

"Of course he does, Mum."

"Are you sure?"

"Yes I'm sure. But you can ask him yourself. He'll be here in the morning."

She did ask him next morning, as soon as he arrived. She was satisfied with his answer.

"She just wants you to be happy," he said, when I asked him about it later.

I wasn't ready to believe that. I was sure Mum wanted only three things from her girls: that we'd look stylish; that we'd behave perfectly; and that we'd grow up to be exactly like her. She didn't seem to know that we were people separate from her. Individuals. Different, perhaps, to what she'd expected, what she thought was normal, natural.

When I left home, I was determined to become the real me—the girl, the woman I'd always known was lurking inside—hidden under those outfits; buried inside that too-responsible big sister; choked down by years of stifling expectations.

I was sure she would be a wild and beautiful creature, bursting with creativity, energy and colour, filled with wide-eyed wonder, infused with magic and spirit. An intrepid adventurer, a powerful yogi, a quiet meditator. A superhero, a life-saver, a champion for the underdog. A plantswoman, a healer. A writer. She would wear a long emerald green velvet dress. Her name would be Susanna.

I expected her to emerge fully fledged, as soon as I left home. She remained a fantasy.

I'm living alone for the first time. Separated, not divorced yet. Mum comes to stay. I feel dull and heavy, like I'm drowning. She shines like the sun and I shrivel. It's nothing she says or does. It's just energy. Hers feels so much stronger than mine.

I coach myself, "Just be an adult with her. Just talk to her like you'd talk to anyone else." But all I can do is shrink away. It's automatic. A sea anemone sucking itself in, disappearing.

I invite some girlfriends over. "Please come and entertain my mother. Bring wine." I sit back in my favourite chair, wondering at their easy conversation and laughter.

"I would hate to have to live alone."

"I don't *have* to, Mum. I want to. I love having my own space."

"You are so like your father."

"Thanks."

"You got all his genes. And none of mine." She smiled. A compliment.

In the dream I was knee-deep in blue water. Dad walked beside me. "Help me die," he pleaded. "I need to be dead before the wedding."

Mum had just married Michael and they were visiting Vancouver. I told them the dream. Michael said, "Sounds like you've still got some work to do."

"Do you want to talk about it?" Mum sounded genuinely concerned.

"No."

It was only two years since Dad had died. I was still in the grips of grief. I wasn't willing to share it with Mum. I wasn't willing to share it with anybody.

I tell Mum about a new boyfriend. Not exactly a boy. He's much older than me—closer to Mum's age. Also, he's married. She listens when I tell her about the strong connection between us. She doesn't say, "But Susan, how could you… " She just nods and listens.

"Would you like to meet him?"

"OK."

We meet for lunch. She's polite and friendly, betrays no disapproval.

She says, after he left the restaurant, "I can see you're happy. That furrow between your brow—the one you've had since you were a baby—it's gone. This is the first time I've seen you without it."

When she's in Vancouver, she keeps her watch on New Zealand time. "The kids are heading off to school now." "The kids will be going to bed." I'm irritated with the running commentary on the grandchildren. I won't be contributing to the grandchild count. One day she changes her watch to local time. "It's quite nice not having to think about children all the time, isn't it? You've got a good life."

The memories of Mum's visits to Vancouver are wispy. They're difficult to drag up, and they are even more difficult to look at honestly. I can see, even in this handful of images, Mum was ready for a different kind of relationship with me. But I kept her shut out.

This is what I'm seeing as I write about her dying. I had steeled myself against her so completely, put on an armour so bulky I was practically immobile. I couldn't get out and she couldn't get in.

When did this all start? Nobody's born recoiling from their mother, are they? When did I first cringe away? I can't remember ever feeling relaxed with her. I can't remember a single intimate happy moment with her. Why not? My curiosity gets the better of me. I get hypnosis.

The therapist walks me back in time. We keep going and going. Back past all the memories, to a time I can't remember. Six months old. That's when I first felt betrayed, abandoned. "The subconscious knows everything, Sue. It doesn't lie." She walks me back from my childhood into the TV room where I'm sitting in the glow of my laptop. Hypnosis by Skype.

There *is* a story from when I was a baby. The shark bite story.

I don't think I knew about the deep scar on the top of my left leg, until I started swimming lessons, and some of the kids laughed at me for having two bum cheeks on one side. The flesh and skin at the top of my left leg pucker deep into a jagged scar. It did look like I had another bum cheek on that side. Still does.

I must have told Mum about the teasing. Her eyes narrowed. One eyebrow arched. She opened her eyes wide, serious.

"Next time someone teases you, tell them you got bitten by a shark at Oreti Beach. That scar is where the shark's teeth went in. Tell them you were lucky your leg wasn't bitten right off. It was a miracle you survived."

I couldn't wait for swimming. "Look at my shark bite!" I showed off the scar to my impressed classmates.

The true story was a routine polio vaccination injection gone wrong. What should have been a quick-healing jab, turned to pus. The doctor came to

cut and clean and drain it. I screamed till I was blue in the face. It took weeks to heal. The doctor couldn't come every day, so it was Mum's job to keep the wound clean and open. The doctor warned her if she didn't keep it open, a deep scar would form on my leg.

My screaming disturbed Mum so much she stopped opening the wound. She said my screaming was too much for her. She couldn't bear to hurt her baby like that.

"She'll have that scar for life," the doctor scolded. He was only thinking about my leg.

I don't mind the scar at all. It only ever bothered me that one time, at the swimming pool, before Mum invented the shark bite story. But I wonder. Was that the start of the fear, the recoiling? When she followed the doctor's orders and pried open the infected wound, did I seize up and shrink from her? Did I stop trusting her? Is it even possible for a baby to experience these things?

Later there were other reasons to shrink away, but maybe it all started with the shark bite. Maybe deep in my subconscious, I believed she was the shark. Maybe.

Mum's fading. She's not going to last much longer. "It will probably be tonight," my aunty whispers when I ask her.

I wish I was writing a work of fiction. This is the part where the daughter would stand up from the rocking chair. She'd sit on the bed, take her mother's frail hands in her own. "Mum, I'm so sorry about how things turned out between us. I don't know why we didn't seem to know how to love each other. I'm so sorry I shut you out. I know you were trying to make things better between us."

The mother would open her eyes and smile her last smile, "None of that matters any more darling. I just want you to be happy."

But neither of us said a word.

Instead I crawled into bed with her, and hung on, until she died.

Chapter 12
ENDINGS

The morning Mum died, my sisters arrived at the house around six o'clock, and we all sat around the kitchen table with nothing to do. It was still dark outside. The house was deadly quiet.

We wait. For what? To call the authorities—someone to take her body away and get it ready for burial. We'd have to face a funeral now. After these weeks of dying, there has to be a big shin-dig. A last hurrah. It was a bit early in the day to call the authorities, so we just sat there.

We did call Nana, Mum's mother. We decided she probably shouldn't drive. Someone went to pick her up.

"Anyone want a cup of tea?"

"How about a gin and tonic?"

"It's six in the morning."

"So? I need something stronger than tea."

We poured a round of gin and tonics. Drank them sourly, without the usual festivity of clinking glasses. It was like we forced it down, to calm our nerves, nothing else.

Someone called Mum's closest family members, her close friends. The engine started to purr. We could feel it. Cars would start pulling up to the curb any minute, their lights in the dim morning gloom would switch off, ten seconds later the doorbell would ring.

"Let's just open the front door wide. It's not cold. I can't stand the sound of that doorbell ringing one more time."

So we opened the front door. Finished our gins and washed out the glasses. Everyone knew the Ward girls were lushes, and we never shied away from that image, but with our mother still warm in her death bed, we felt slightly ashamed. But we were fortified. Ready. For what, we didn't really know.

At eight o'clock, I phoned the undertaker. They were expecting our call; they would pick her up at nine. Like a taxi, going to town for a spot of shopping.

"If you want her dressed in anything special, have it ready for when we come."

I'd better pack her a bag, I thought, and went up to her room. Wish I'd done it yesterday.

Mum was lying where I'd left her, a couple of hours ago. No life in her at all. No chance there'd been a mistake and she just passed out for a spell. Dead. Still, like she had never been in life. Statue still.

She looked peaceful, but so old. Older than her own mother.

I found an overnight bag in the bottom of her closet. I pulled her navy wedding dress off its hanger and folded it into the bag. Won't matter if it's a bit crumpled. Should I pack shoes? She liked heels, just low ones so she didn't tower over her husband. Either of them. She'd had two husbands, neither of them much taller than she was. She limited her heels to an inch and a half, max. Maybe she doesn't need shoes.

Will she need underwear? I could hardly pack her off without it. I pulled open the smaller drawers of the big antique wood dresser. Scarves. T-shirts. Belts and bags. Bras and undies—the sorriest selection of bras and undies I'd seen in a long time. Old, misshapen. I knew Mum wouldn't be extravagant about underwear, but I felt sure she'd have a better selection than this rag bag. The only half decent set I could find was a faded dark blue bra—almost, but not quite a sports bra, and some big undies almost the same colour. I scrounged through the other drawers; that was the best I could find. It would have to do. I supposed the undertaker had seen worse.

I zipped up the bag and put it on the floor at the foot of the bed. I felt bad about that underwear.

The undertaker arrived with a trolley on wheels, folded neatly so it slipped in the front door and up the narrow hallway easily.

"Is there another way out of the house?" he asked as they unfolded it beside Mum's bed.

"The patio door and out through the garden, down the neighbour's driveway. There's nobody home there at the moment. Or through the garage. There's no car in there."

"It would be better if you left the room now."

I went back to the kitchen. When I heard a bang in the hallway five minutes later, I opened the kitchen door, and looked around the corner up the hall. They had the trolley standing on one end, manoeuvring it around a small table with a huge flower arrangement on it. Mum was strapped in firmly with some big seat-belts. But her head was loose, jerked forward and swaying with the trolley as they navigated it around the tight corner.

"Can't you take her out through the garden?"

The undertakers jolted around, surprised. "The garage will be quicker. We'll call you when she's ready for viewing."

"She didn't look like that before she got sick. She was really pretty."

"We'll take care of it."

"Don't forget the bag of clothes. Does she need shoes?"

"No. No shoes."

As they drove the gleaming black hearse away, I thought of all the times Mum had said, "Never leave the house with holes in your socks or underwear—in case you get in an accident and have to go to the hospital."

A couple of days later, we were going through her room, cleaning up, looking for things to keep, things to give to her friends, her sisters. I pulled open the bottom drawer of her bedside table. It was full of underwear. Elegant, stylish, just the right amount of lace, matching sets. Of all the finds, that day, this was the hardest. A side of my mother I knew existed, but I didn't find until after she was gone.

My sisters and I arrived at the funeral home ten minutes after the undertaker called. We wanted to be the first to see her. The undertaker showed us into the room, then left. One of us closed the door behind him.

"Mum would never wear blue eye shadow. That's got to go." Maria whipped out her makeup bag, and got to work on Mum's cold eyelids, removing the cheap shimmery funeral home blue and replacing it with a dusty grey green, Mum's colour.

"That's better."

"And she'd never wear her hair behind her ears like that."

"Have we got any hair spray?" We hadn't thought to bring it. So we pulled the hair from behind her ears and did our best to comb it into a decent bob. It wasn't great, but it was better.

"Do you think the undertaker will notice?"

"Who cares? We've got to make her look half decent for her own funeral."

Her hands seemed a bit creepy, so we tried to move them but they were locked together in prayer, and that's where they had to stay.

I don't remember if we brought her perfume to spritz her hair and shoulders. I hope we did.

We stepped back.

"She looks just like a doll."

We carried her from the hearse into the church, her five daughters and her youngest brother. The night before a Catholic funeral, there's a Rosary. Next to Good Friday afternoon service, Rosaries are the worst. They go on and on, around and around the Rosary beads, one mumbled Hail Mary after another, and I just can't see the point. Except it gives you something to do.

A funeral gives you plenty to do. You need to pick a day and time. You need to pick songs from the hymn book, nothing too morbid, but not too joyful either. You need to get an organist, and find someone to do the flowers for the church. Who's going to do the readings? Who's going to speak about Mum and her life? What are they going to say?

Then there's the programme for the Requiem Mass. An 8.5 x 11 folded booklet with the words to the hymns and readings, and a picture of the deceased on the front. Catholics save these things to remember their dead. It needs to be a good picture.

We were back at the photo box again, not wandering down memory lane, but shuffling through all the photos trying to find one of Mum suitable for a funeral programme. Clearly our mother hadn't had her own funeral in mind when she posed for the camera. In every shot she was acting the goat or raising a wine glass in front of her face.

"There's got to be one serious photo of her. One shot where she looks normal."

"Well I can't find one."

"OK, we need to look through again. If we could just find a good one of her face, we could crop it."

And that's what we did. Mum's dressed as a can-can girl in her funeral photo. She's at a fancy-dress ball, beaming, alive and well, acting up for the camera. Her wine glass was far enough away from her face that we could crop it out and not wreck the photo.

Everyone said it was their favourite funeral photo ever. Everyone said that's exactly the picture she would have picked.

But in her coffin—the lid was open during the Rosary—she looked serious. People shuffled up the aisle to the front of the church, to look at her. Why do we do that? To make sure they really are dead? To make sure we really understand they're gone? They are gone. That's for sure. There's nothing ambiguous about a dead body.

My mother's body was utterly vacated. She was gone, and we were sitting in a church pew beside her empty shell. At least her eye shadow was the right colour. Relatives, friends, strangers filed past the box, looked in. Some spoke to her in quiet mumbles, some dabbed their eyes. Some reached in and touched her head.

We sat in a row, looking ahead, looking down. It's so hard to feel anything.

The priest and the funeral director put the lid on the coffin after the Rosary service. They leave the body in the church overnight, alone and silent. Then we all come back for the funeral the next day.

I feel bad about leaving Mum in the church overnight. She'd have hated that. The cold silence. Being alone.

But we had to go back to the house. We had to greet people, serve food, pour drinks. Another thing to occupy us. We had to go home and listen to people gushing over our dead mother. And our dead father. They will want to take photos of the five Ward girls, all in a row, just like when we were kids.

"Maybe we should have got matching outfits for the funeral."

"Yeah, that would have made Mum's day."

Next day we carried her coffin from the hearse to the graveside. Dad's grave. It was the only plot in the cemetery with a rough green river rock headstone. Mum had spent weeks searching the Arrow River for that rock. Dad's grave had been dug up, to make room for Mum. There was straw at the bottom, and we could see right through it to Dad's coffin, ten years in the ground. I wonder if he's a skeleton yet? I bet his white curly hair is still there, still so soft.

We stood around and looked in. Mum and Dad. Dum and Mad. Dead.

The priests prayed, sprayed holy water, waved the incense, and pushed the secret button so Mum's coffin rolled, gently, down into the cold ground, right on top of Dad. The priest threw in a clod of dirt.

We threw in flowers, roses from her garden, enough for both of them.

Epilogue

Mum,

The other night I lay tilted right back on the deck chair, looking up through the greenhouse roof at the black sky. It's May, and it's still freezing cold. I was wrapped up in a thick wool blanket—one I took from your linen cupboard years ago. I was thinking about you. Again.

I'd just finished the final draft of my book. I have thought about you so much, in so much detail, as I've made myself remember and write down these stories. I feel like you've been with me for the past five years. I know you better now.

I know now, beyond a doubt, you weren't the villain I'd always thought you were. You were wounded. You wanted to protect your girls from the things you suffered as a child. I get that. You went way too far overboard, but I get it.

I also know, beyond a doubt, how thoroughly I locked you out. I wouldn't give you a crumb of myself, not a scrap of intimacy, even though I knew that's what you really wanted. Maybe that's what I wanted too. I would give anything for it now.

When I sat at your bedside for those three weeks before you died, I couldn't bust out of my fear of you, couldn't crack open even a tiny bit. I can see you, lying there, dying. I see myself in the old rocking chair watching you, watching over you. It is such a sorrowful scene. Not because of what we were about to lose; but because we'd spent almost our whole lives resisting, opposing each other. And neither of us could break that spell.

I lay in my deck chair looking up at the sky, thinking and feeling all this.

Then I saw you. It really was like a vision. Like you appeared to me, on purpose. You were in the distance, but I could see you clearly. You looked beautiful. Your face was bright and carefree. You stood still and looked at me for a few long moments. Not a threatening look, a kind, searching look.

I thought you were going to come towards me, and I didn't know what would happen—maybe we'd hug, or talk. But you didn't come. You turned and started to walk toward a big door with a bright light shining behind it. Then you stopped and turned your head. Your hair swung, jaunty, and you shot me the warmest, most genuine smile I've ever seen from you. Like you knew this was it—our struggle was over—we're free of each other.

You walked through the door, and it shut behind you.

You were gone for good. Free.

I'm sure you were telling me I'm free too.

Here's something I didn't know until now. All this time, you were my muse. You gave me every one of these unlikely stories.

This is our book.

Acknowledgements

I want to say a big thanks to:

David, for listening patiently to my childhood stories, and saying, "It's amazing you turned out so normal."

My sisters, Julie, Polly, Maria and Ange. You've all helped in all sorts of ways, to unravel some murky memories, straighten out the facts, and fill in missing details. And thanks also for being such amazing sisters.

My first ever writing group, Josephine Granese, Charlotte Schuckard, and Hilary Wilke. You wonderful women encouraged me to get much more personal with my writing when I was feeling very afraid of trying to write a memoir. I am very grateful to you three for getting me started.

The writers who meet at the round table at Acadia University every Friday to read and critique works in progress. Without that weekly meeting, and without your excellent feedback and encouragement, I would never have finished this book. I'm especially grateful to Muriel Zimmer and Kathy France, fellow memoir writers, for our weekly writing sessions in the Garden Room. Just being in your orbit keeps me inspired.

The friends, particularly Lotta Dann, Charlotte Schuckard, Michele Westlaken, and Jennifer Stanley, who've been willing readers and always encouraged me to keep on writing.

Vivienne Elder-Smith and Leanne Babcock both read the manuscript and offered valuable feedback.

Jo Constable, thanks for a perfect and gorgeous cover design.

Matt Clairmont, thank you for inspiring me to take the self-publishing route, and for guiding me expertly through that process.

SK

About the Author

Sue was five years old, sitting cross-legged on the floor of the Invercargill Public Library, listening to the children's librarian reading *Rain Makes Applesauce,* when she knew she wanted to write books.

She has written since she was little, mostly personal, quiet writing—diaries, poems, letters. After a 30-year career as an editor and writer, helping hundreds of people find their voices, tell their stories and publish their writing, Sue decided it was time to write her own stories, in her own voice.

It's more than 50 years since that epiphany in the library. *Unlikely Stories of a Perfect Childhood* is Sue's first book. She reckons it won't be her last.

Sue Kerr is a Kiwi-Canadian living in Wolfville, Nova Scotia. She will always think of Invercargill, New Zealand as home. You can contact Sue at www.suekerr.ca.

Photo credit: Jordan Siobhan, Nostalgic Photography, Wanaka, New Zealand. @nostalgic_photography_nz

www.ingramcontent.com/pod-product-compliance
Ingram Content Group UK Ltd.
Pitfield, Milton Keynes, MK11 3LW, UK
UKHW020417250726
13967UKWH00007B/2688

9 781999 147204